Emails

From

Hell

Evil schemes to undermine leaders

OTHER BOOKS BY MATT RAWLINS

"THE QUESTION" SERIES
The Question
The Namer

OTHERS PENDING
The Container
The Expression
The Classroom
The Conversation
The Line
The View
The Choice
The Gate & other short stories

LEADERSHIP BOOKS PENDING
Managing to learn,
Learning to manage

Communicating to learn,
Learning to communicate

Cultural diversity in learning,
Learning in cultural diversity

Emails From Hell

Evil schemes to undermine leaders

Matt Rawlins

AMuzement Publications
Salem, Oregon

Library of Congress Catalog Card Number: 99-90279

Acknowledgments

The inspiration for this book is the writing of C. S. Lewis who went to be with the Lord in 1963. I have read and reread his works of brilliance and they have had a profound influence on my life. I would never attempt to imitate his work; it's simply not possible. In his book "The Screwtape Letters" he writes of a senior demon's letters to a junior demon, Wormwood, on how to tempt and mislead a young man. As my research and work is with leaders and organizations, I have used a similar format to explore how the demonic world tempts and destroys leaders and organizations in our day. I have gone so far as to change the spelling of Wormwood to Wyrmwud to put distance between our writing. Think of my Wyrmwud as the great, great grandson of Lewis' Wormwood.

I would be the first to acknowledge the difference between my writing and C. S. Lewis'. I hope there is no comparison made for I know how I will end up. I do hope that his work will stand for him and mine will stand for me and that each will give glory to the same creative God we have both loved and served.

No book is the work of just one person. So it is with this book. There are many to thank. This could not have been done without the help of a brilliant editor and friend, Sandi Tompkins, and a small weekly writers group that includes: Ross Tooley, Marge Clewett, Yolanda Olson, Roxanne Olson, Douglas and Margaret Feaver, and Audra Jo Baumgarth (thanks for the countless bowls of popcorn). Finally, a big thank you to Dr. Duane Rawlins, my dad, who has helped in more ways than I can count to make this possible.

Dedication

To my wife Celia and my son Joshua.
Thank you for everything.

Table of disContents

Our Wicked Ways -- The Goal

Strategies For Luring Leaders To Destruction

Twisting Things Our Way

The Weapons At Your Disposal

Dealing With Our Enemy

Appendix

Preface

Be aware that the devil is the Father of Lies and thus not everything that is contained in these emails is true. It is assumed that his perception of the world is bent and any explanation he offers or how he views the people in this story will be twisted to his perspective.

What can be said is that the devil does have a strategy and is clearly at work to bring about our destruction. I don't think it is because we are so valuable in ourselves, but rather that he wants to get back at his enemy and knows we are the soft spot in his enemy's heart. He knows any pain he brings on us is pain brought to the one he vehemently hates. We have played a role in evil's place in our world, and it seems to be in our best interest to be aware of what the plans of the devil are.

By some quirk of cyberspace and unknown quantum space physics these emails appeared in my IN basket periodically over these last years. That is the only explanation I have for how I received them.

From: <Wyrmwud> wyrmwud@hell.edu
To: <Tweazel> tweazel@hell.edu
Subject: <u>Our Focus</u>

Tweazel,

Just a short note to review my position on your
work. As you well know, with the population
growth in this century, there are now too many
humans for us to be able to watch over each
one. Our Founder Below foresaw this years ago
and thus our focus has been solely on those
who will be leaders or who are already leaders.
Even with this strategy we are stretched to
keep up. For this reason, although you have
not performed very well in recent years, you
were entrusted a young subject to watch over.

Please don't underestimate the risk I have
taken in giving you this opportunity. It was not
without great peril to me and I can assure you
if you make mistakes, I will not be the one to
pay for them. I would like periodic reports on
your young subject's growth and leadership.

Your observing friend,
Wyrmwud

From: <Wyrmwud> wyrmwud@hell.edu
To: <Tweazel> tweazel@hell.edu
Subject: <u>Shame</u>

Tweazel,

Your brief note was helpful and I am encouraged to believe there is hope for you in our
ranks. I would hate to see you stuck at the
bottom of our organization, forever at the beck
and call of every whim of our fraternity. I think
we will be able to work together and you
might eventually fit into my organization.

Your work at shaming your very young subject
is a great idea. It has been one of our strongest,
most effective tools ever since the human scum
joined our side in the fight against our enemy.
Using an older girl to take advantage of him
can only work to our advantage. Remind him
of the brief pleasure it was, even if the pleasure
was to be needed by someone else, so that he
takes some level of responsibility for it. Although you didn't say, I am trusting she was
the ugly neighbor who lives close by and is
seen often by him. This will enable you to
reinforce the shame every time he sees her.

Our enemy has placed a desire in all human
scum to be responsible. Exploit it. Leaders
seem to be extremely sensitive to this and you
must constantly be twisting and distorting
their ideas about responsibility. Rarely is love

born from responsibility. With some work, responsibility usually brings forth legalism and conformity. Young subjects are particularly vulnerable and the more painful experiences you can build into their lives the better, as they have not developed the tools or strength to know how to deal with them. A long-term strategy is to make them responsible for everything. With painful experiences and the weight of the world on their shoulders, they learn to accept leadership and twist it for their own purposes.

Having said that, there is another side I have found to be just as effective. Have your subject get hurt and associate the pain with leading. With some influence on your part he will avoid leadership because of the pain involved. I would encourage you to watch your young subject and see what his natural tendency is and then use this against him. We want a subject who must have leadership in order to justify his existence or a leader who will give it up in a second as soon as it gets difficult. What we don't want is a leader who is just as comfortable following as leading. This works against many of our most subtle influences and will make your job much more difficult.

One final thought on painful experiences. We have found over the years there are many benefits to our side in helping them push the experiences down and letting them get locked into their subconscious minds. As this happens they will be in similar situations and not know why they are reacting. If you work this specific situation with your subject right, he will constantly struggle to trust other female vermin. You must convince him that they all want to use him. Don't make it a conscious thought, just a feeling that is deep down within him.

As he gets a little older have him talk about it with some friends and make sure they laugh at him. This will add fuel to the pain and as his reasoning powers grow, you can twist his ideas and beliefs and he will never even question the pain. It becomes a foundation upon which much of our work is based. These hidden caves of pain can be very useful for later years when he will find the advantages of power to protect himself. These painful experiences create a vacuum that will suck all the power he can find into it as a way to get false comfort or to protect himself.

Your watchful friend,
Wyrmwud

From: <Wyrmwud> wyrmwud@hell.edu
To: <Tweazel> tweazel@hell.edu
Subject: <u>Killing simulators</u>

Tweazel,

Your focus on using killing simulators or what
the vermin would call video games is good
preparation for the future. However, you don't
seem to grasp the strategy we have for these
games. Let me help you see the beauty of our
goals.

We have been able to mask what the vermin
would call the pain and horror of killing and
have made it a game for the children. We want
them to be able to kill quickly and get used to
destroying the competition without any viola-
tion of conscience so that later as leaders, it will
be natural to destroy any opposition. The
child's first innocent impression is quickly
overruled by intrigue and the challenge the
game offers. They quickly become desensitized
to fighting and even gather pleasure in killing
as many as possible. After all, it's just a game.

A word of caution, do not get your hopes up
that we will be able to turn millions of children
into mass murderers because of the games. Oh,
that it would be so simple. We know we can
only turn a few, but the consequences will be
worth it. Overall our desire is to desensitize
them and create destructive mechanisms for

dealing with challenges. Leaders who seek to win through destroying others offer us some of our richest opportunities.

On a side note, some of our tech heads and visionaries argue that we will soon be able to offer them a virtual world where all their lusts can be met. This will provide a wonderful escape from their painful real world and will give them the illusion they don't have to deal with it. They will be able to create their own world and thus will feed the illusion that they are gods.

Don't expect quick results with the games. Be patient.

Your patient friend,
Wyrmwud

From: <Wyrmwud> wyrmwud@hell.edu
To: <Tweazel> tweazel@hell.edu
Subject: <u>Your subject's opportunity</u>

Tweazel,

It has come to my attention that your subject has broken up some of the younger kids fighting and as a result he has been given a position of leadership in a local youth organization. I despise how he attained the leadership but for your sake, it is about time. Any form of leadership is better to work with then none at all. I was wondering whether you were going to be able to produce a leader out of your work or whether I might have to remove you from your position. We expect all our subjects to have leadership influence by their last year of high school.

I am also aware that you are talking with some of the other fraternity members about my counsel to you. Let me assure you Tweazel that I will hear about all you say and do. As you have begun to use my name and raise the smallest questions about whether my ideas will work, could it be that you do not understand how much you need me and my help in this fraternity? Do you not understand the influence I have and how much I know? Let me assure you, you will need my help if you are to survive and you will not get it by questioning others about me.

Now, to the point of work at hand. You mentioned that you were prompting your young subject to talk about some of his problems to his friends. This is a very dangerous route to take and I would give the strongest caution. I did say to share with some friends, but only those he feels inferior to and desperately wants to impress. See to it that he only shares this with other subjects who will laugh at him or in some way belittle him. If you did not learn this in school be sure you get it right this time. Any exposure of his heart before others without some set up for more pain is a great loss to you. If he thinks he can expose his inner thoughts and feelings with friends and they will listen, this will rob you of the power to use those hidden things against him.

As you seem to have clearly missed what I was saying earlier, I will make this simple for you. Leaders must not deal with issues of their own hearts. They must be driven by them but never allowed to expose them or see them outside the filtering effect of painful emotions. Any opportunity for the young leader to expose his heart must only be in the context of you working with one of our fraternity members to make sure someone uses it against him. Set him up with his friends as they are sitting around, bored and not knowing what to do. Let your subject risk talking about what happened with the ugly female vermin in his youth who used him to fulfill her own lusts. Instead of his friends understanding, have his friends twist it quickly. Get them to tease him, "Wussy, can't even protect yourself from a girl." "You're whining about that? What a wimp! Some ladies man you are." Have them create a nickname like 'wimpy' that mocks him and then have them use it against him for years.

When your young leader shares openly with others, and they don't make fun of him, then you lose some of the authority these experiences have over him. Our enemy has made the human parasites in such a way that exposing themselves to others actually gives them more of themselves back. Do not expect me to explain this as some of our best filthosophers have been working around this for centuries. It is not something that we dare attempt to play with. Your feeble little mind should just leave it alone.

Your powerful friend,
Wyrmwud

From: <Wyrmwud> wyrmwud@hell.edu
To: <Tweazel> tweazel@hell.edu
Subject: <u>Comparison</u>

Tweazel,

I see you are using my ideas to good effect on your subject. I am particularly pleased to hear that you have continued to work on his concept of responsibility. In addition to this, I would encourage you to highlight the personality, abilities and strengths of those he works with. You mentioned another leader that many of the younger vermin look up to. Let your subject see his own differences from this leader as weaknesses. He will not be consciously aware of his own strengths any more than he is aware of his own breathing. Strengths are often natural abilities that the vermin don't have to work at. He will assume that if it is so easy for him then it can't be a strength.

Point out others operating in their strengths, so he will feel like he has a weakness. Is the other leader decisive? If he is then belittle your subject as being too indecisive. If someone else is funny, then make him feel like he is boring. If nothing else works, highlight physical differences and use them against your subject. Open the door for comparison. Tie it together with his wanting to be responsible. Pour on the condemnation as he will sense his own responsibility to be like the other leaders he admires and will find out very quickly that he can't be like them. Comparison is a wonderful way to open his eyes to what you will convince him are his weaknesses. This opens the door for two of our most powerful allies as comparison can awaken within him Envy and Jealousy.

In the early days of our learning to influence man, we saw the power of this with Cain and Abel. Cain could not stand the comparison with his brother. When he saw himself in the light of his brother's offering, it was easier for him to destroy his brother than accept the reality of his own weaknesses. We knew then that this would be a powerful ally, one that has been used with thousands of leaders who have joined us. Never let them be comfortable with themselves. You will remember how effectively it was used to destroy the hated one who came to earth. It was Envy and Jealousy in the heart of the religious leaders of the time that allowed us to attack the hated one. You can see the power of this as they were supposed to be his very own slaves. Yet the seeds of Envy and Jealousy were planted deep in them as they could not stand the comparison. It was easy to turn them against the hated one after they compared themselves to him. You must always remember that the human scum, and especially leaders, do not like to see themselves as weak, limited or lacking.

Your much-needed friend,
Wyrmwud

From: <Wyrmwud> wyrmwud@hell.edu
To: <Tweazel> tweazel@hell.edu
Subject: <u>Missions statement</u>

Tweazel,

I just had a meeting with Our Founder Below and he nearly consumed us for what he called, slacking off. Our Founder Below has sensed some distractions in the fraternity and has dictated that every member in our fraternity say the missions statement hourly until it has been burned into our minds. Repeat after me:

"Our mission is to attack, destroy, defame, slander, smear, blame, insult, slur, dishonor, belittle, criticize, denounce, berate, castigate, lie about and find fault with the nature and character of our enemy."

If by chance you would attempt to get off the hook by feigning ignorance as to the nature and character of our enemy, let me say it clearly. His nature has to do with his greatness, character has to do with his goodness. As a result of your work, this will always translate into an understanding your subject has that the enemy is not big enough or good enough to require 100 percent commitment from him.

Having made that clear, this and this alone is the standard upon which all your actions will be judged. It is the basis of authority and promotion in our fraternity and the foundation upon which all our work is built. DO NOT FORGET IT FOR ONE MOMENT. Your very survival hangs on your capacity to accomplish this in and through your subject.

Your motivated friend,
Wyrmwud

From: <Wyrmwud> wyrmwud@hell.edu
To: <Tweazel> tweazel@hell.edu
Subject: <u>Leadership</u>

Tweazel,

As I have had some time to observe you I have sensed you are not the smartest member in my organization. Therefore, I thought I better explain why it is important to destroy the nature and character of our enemy.

Our enemy declares he genuinely likes the human vermin and has gone as far as to state that he wants a relationship with them. (Although we question his integrity in making such a ridiculous statement, we have found no other reason for his interest in them.) In order to have a relationship he has given them free will. That means he has limited his leadership over them to influence. So the deep dark question is, what is it about our enemy that influences the human scum?

The answer is, his nature and character. The willingness of humanity to follow our enemy's leadership is solely dependent on how well they know him. The clearer they see him, the more they will follow him. The less they know about him, the more open they are to us. You can see this clearly in Our Founder Below's brilliant influence over Adam and Eve as he simply helped them to see that our enemy was selfish and didn't want what was best for them. Once they saw this they immediately defected to our side. This battle for influence, my dear Tweazel, is what the war is all about.

As I am writing I realize you might think that this pertains only to our enemy. No, this is the foundation for all leadership. In order for somebody to lead, they must convince others that they have power and/or want what is best for those following them. Let me try to make this as practical as possible. You have mentioned that the overall leader of the youth organization is an old man who is hard of hearing. Your subject has tried to talk with him and he isn't sure the old man could understand everything he said. This provides an opportunity for you. You can begin to play with your subject's thoughts, *How can an old man know what is best for us? How can he even understand us if he can't hear us? If he can't hear, maybe his brain is not working so well either. He probably doesn't even know what is going on around here.* However small and subtle the thoughts are, they break the link of influence the older man has over your subject. If the old buzzard is neither big enough (knows what is best to do) nor good enough (wants what is best for them) in your subject's eyes, then he will not be influenced by his leadership.

Remember, if you want your leader to succeed and have influence and thus leadership, you must always have him put on this facade of knowing what to do and wanting what is best for those involved. I am sure you will have noticed that is just what the enemy tried to do with us and is trying to do with the human scum.

Now having said that, it seems you are beginning to work with your subject's feelings, but I want you to use more energy in this area. A particular opening is when there is pain, suffering or injustice. This is the time when you want his mind to be most active, when it is full of these emotions. During this time of pain, he will come to conclusions that will be distorted. Continue pushing haunting images of starving children, wars in other parts of the world, the suffering of those being attacked by other wonderfully hideous vermin there or the injustices that his friends face. Use these to disturb your subject.

Remember, our enemy made these little snot-nosed creatures to seek meaning. You must work with the way they are made, turn this desire for meaning against them when the understanding needed is not intellectual, but emotional. Influence them to want an emotional answer that will subtly twist their reasoning. We know only their faith can bring an answer, but convince them to demand understanding through their own thinking process. Tell your subject that an intellectual answer that naively states the enemy is good, when your subject has such strong feelings of injustice, is hypocrisy on his part and too simplistic. If he accepts this reasoning, you have him.

When your subject is not emotionally involved, do not stir him to wrestle with difficult issues for he can find answers much easier when he is not seduced by his emotions. Do your best work with anger, suffering and injustice. A strong kick while he is feeling down is worth a thousand kicks when he is feeling good. Do not let him just settle the pain with faith in who our enemy is.

If for any reason your subject comes to the final and never-to-be questioned conclusion that our enemy is good and in control, then your work is over. The enemy will put a shield around him and your influence will be lost. Your only hope is to never let him come to that statement of faith. If you do, consider yourself my next meal.

Your scheming friend,
Wyrmwud

From: <Wyrmwud> wyrmwud@hell.edu
To: <Tweazel> tweazel@hell.edu
Subject: <u>Radical</u>

Tweazel,

Your idea of wanting your subject in his youthful zeal to be radical is a good attack. But you must be careful not to let him find out what the meaning of radical is. It seems the enemy has put within each new generation a desire to be radical. So your desire to misdirect it can only help our work. Make him think of this word as a destruction of what exists, the removal of all the 'old' useless things built by those who have gone before him.

Do not let him find out that radical actually means "root." Thus if he were to be radical it would actually mean for him to get to the root of things. The foundations. Anyone who thinks deeply about fundamentals will be by definition radical and thus draw from a power in the enemy that we cannot fight. He always wants to take them to the basics and seems to always reward those who continually watch over this. We must misdirect this focus so they want to do something completely new and think they have to build the foundation themselves in a new place, or try and destroy the existing foundations. Push for either of these extremes. Do not let him think that there is a root that is in all the enemy's work and he is to find it and draw from it.

There is something delicious in seeing the life work of aging leaders destroyed, all in the name of being radical. The older man who pioneered the youth organization would be a good example. If the enemy has accomplished some good through this leader, this is a great way to destroy it and bring it to naught. Get the young leaders, all in the name of being radical, to think they have to tear down his work. It is a pleasure I want you to taste so that you hunger more for this kind of destruction.

As a side note, if your subject is not of the strength to destroy the work of others, you will have to develop within him a blind conformity to the traditions of those who have gone before. Don't let him think he can be radical just by understanding what others did and why they did it. Let him try and duplicate it without any understanding and it will produce an organization you can be proud of. One that is ineffective, rule-bound and dead. I will write more on this later as you are not yet ready for it.

Your radical friend,
Wyrmwud

From: <Wyrmwud> wyrmwud@hell.edu
To: <Tweazel> tweazel@hell.edu
Subject: <u>Equality</u>

Tweazel,

While you are on this area of justice I have
found a very useful trick that you may want to
employ with your young subject. It involves
twisting issues in such a way as to hide what
the enemy is doing. Here's an example to help
your feeble little mind understand:

One of our enemy's zealous little fools was
upset over the pain of injustice and racial
prejudice. So he created a slogan that said,
"Love sees no color." That idea quickly
spawned a movement. These misguided vermin were trying to show that they are all of the
same race. I joined with Boilstay, and we developed a plan to use this to our good. Those who
started this slogan wanted others to see
through the unique colors to a deeper unity
that all the human scum could have -- that all
were made in the image of the enemy. I believe
it was their intention to get the scum bags to
recognize that they were all together in this, so
that if they were hurting others, they were in
fact hurting themselves.

With some careful planning and subtle twisting
of words we have used this to our advantage. I
must confess it was the basis of my promotion.

It took our leaders a while to see my wisdom, but in the end they finally did.

The enemy's goal was to help the human vermin see that colors were an expression of a deeper image they bear. This would put their eyes on the hated one and not themselves or us, and could not be allowed to happen. I began working with key subjects and we changed the emphasis. We pointed out that color was the problem and that there should be no color.

This way they came to the conclusion that there could be no appreciation for differences among themselves. In the end, they focused on removing anything that makes them unique, all in the name of justice and love. Anyone who talks about color is considered politically incorrect because it is seen as discrimination.

Thus, different expressions of beauty become an inequality that must be dealt with and removed. Beauty is removed in the name of prejudice and we have turned a momentary insight from our enemy into a slogan for distortion. In recent years we have been able to move beyond the color of their skin and convinced some that any element of uniqueness or beauty is wrong. Bring into their minds that fairness means equality. That equality means that they should all be treated exactly the same, because they all should have the same gifts and abilities. That way if people feel they are unique in some way, then they will feel guilty about it and won't accept it because it will mean the enemy is unfair or they are making others feel bad by their uniqueness. If they do express their uniqueness then get others to quickly rise up and drag them down to the lowest level, again all in the name of justice.

Your wise friend,
Wyrmwud

From: <Wyrmwud> wyrmwud@hell.edu
To: <Tweazel> tweazel@hell.edu
Subject: <u>Hate crime</u>

Tweazel,

You seemed to grasp what I was talking about
in earlier emails and your coercing your subject
to speak behind the other younger leader's
back is encouraging. I have wrestled with the
idea of letting you in on my latest strategy and
have decided to take an immeasurable risk and
invite you to work with me on a new project. I
am currently developing a new strategy to
pervert crime. Here is my plan.

I want you to begin to plant the seeds in your
subject now so that as he grows in influence he
will not see the subtlety of the plan. Let him
hear the phrase 'hate crime' and become familiar with the sound of it. Let him think that hate
crime is just a harsher word for crime and try
to link it with ghastly and hideous crimes. No
one will disagree with that.

I am currently at work to develop within
leaders a hatred for hatred. Don't question this,
as silly as it sounds some of my subjects have
already accepted it. I have publicized and
promoted the deaths of those deliciously mur-
dered because they were homosexuals or
abortion doctors. I have tried to make the
crime more heinous than just a normal killing

as if hatred is a worse poison than other expressions of murder. My subjects seem to accept this without any problem. There is a very subtle and yet growing awareness of how ugly hate crimes are. Tie it to World War II and the treatment of Jews. This may take some time but be patient. True cultural betrayal does not happen overnight.

At the same time I am also working with Smitjoy's subject, a legislator I might add, who is particularly harsh against any form of hatred as expressed in a crime. I am trying to get specific legislation passed against hate crime. Once this happens I will then begin to link hatred to prejudice. I want them to think that any form of prejudice is a budding form of hatred and then to assume that all hatred must be stopped at this early stage before it matures.

During this time I am also at work to highlight subjects who are under our control but claim they are with the enemy's camp. We are pushing these subjects to set out in their hatred to destroy others. The two key areas, as I mentioned, are homosexuality and abortion. Don't let your subject see that although the enemy speaks out against these actions he then foolishly declares he cares about the people who commit them. It's so easy to twist the idea that they are to actually love the person and hate what they are doing. It's laughable really.

At the right time, here is the connection the fraternity wants to make. We will show that the enemy's slaves are promoters of prejudice, intolerance, bigotry and discrimination against others. They talk about hating homosexuality and abortions and thus are actually promoting hatred.

With our legislation in place we will be able to use it against the enemy's slaves as the promoters of prejudice in the world and thus the source of the problem. I will be able to influence key leaders to see that the enemy's slaves are the only ones who have this foolish standard. Be careful. Don't let them think the standard is supposed to be for their own good.

Then I will work in their minds to think that if they could just get rid of those slaves who judge the world, there will be no hatred. Thus in the name of good, our subjects will destroy the work of the enemy's slaves and eventually each other, never realizing it is our work they are doing.

Be very careful with this as it is a delicate work and I will base my next promotion on it. You may work with me on it, but don't do anything unless you consult with me about it first. I don't want to move too quickly and blow our cover.

A good argument from the enemy's slaves could bring this all down if we don't create enough emotion and acceptance of the ideas first.

Your intelligent friend,
Wyrmwud

From: \<Wyrmwud> wyrmwud@hell.edu
To: \<Tweazel> tweazel@hell.edu
Subject: <u>Betrayal</u>

Tweazel,

I wondered why many of your recent notes were so trivial and much about nothing. I assumed you were just refining weaknesses within your subject, but it seems I was misled. You were in trouble and kept your struggles from me. I got a blistering email from Our Exalted Founder Below this morning. He is enraged that your subject has gone over to the enemy's side.

You stupid, miserable, destitute, vile little parasite. I can't believe you didn't contact me as soon as you were aware something was wrong. I was trying to give you an advanced understanding in destroying your subject and you couldn't even get the basics right. You are a moron. I overestimated your abilities and that will not happen again. How completely repulsed and nauseated I am at the thought of it. You withheld from me any clues that this was happening. I cannot begin to explain how hungry this makes me and how you will have to pay for this.

Let me guess what happened. You let him get too close to one of the enemy's slaves. You know the human leeches are usually turned from us through a relationship with someone in the enemy's camp. You let your young subject share his vile little heart and you allowed someone, the old man I bet, sit next to him, put his disgusting arm around him, listen and pretend like he understood. This probably happened several times and you got scared. I would even go as far as to say the old man reached out and acted like he cared. You probably thought the old man could do no damage. I am sure you didn't even check the records to know if he was on our hit list. I am aware that some of the old leaders are not watched as closely. His guardian, Smear, who oversees 25 old buzzards has had little time for him. You should have checked the files to know how wary to be of him. The old buzzards can be the most cunning of all the human parasites.

You are aware that one leader is worth thousands of the souls that will follow him or her. Immeasurable damage has been done and I am outraged that you have kept this from me. I want a hundred copies of our mission statement written out in your own handwriting on my desk by the morning.

Know this, I will keep a closer watch on you in the future through my own network. I am tempted to ask Our Exalted Founder himself to visit you but I do not think you would be of much good to the fraternity if that happened. I know his visitations make a permanent impression. When he is finished, I guarantee you will be motivated.

You must be more careful now as your subject will have access to understanding that will make your work harder. However, be assured we have been working on plans for decades and leaders are the most susceptible to our plans and attacks. We have used many of them for our good all in the name of religion. Wars have been fought and thousands recruited all in the name of extending the enemy's kingdom.

Your note about trying to bring division and chaos in his organization shows that you are still in primary school in your ability to truly use this leader in the more subtle ways of our work. I have noticed that you are hoping to develop an Idi Amin, Pol Pot, Mao Tse Tung or an Adolf Hitler. You secretly crave the blood lust and damage that you can do. The thought of the torture and pain you can cause to our enemy by this attack and blatant destruction is a thought that is close to your heart. I am aware that it is a feeling that all of us draw strength from. To see leaders of destruction up close and to have free access to any destructive action you want is as close to nirvana as we can get without actually doing it ourselves. Just thinking of this stirs me up, but I best get back to the work at hand.

I can't blame you for wanting to retaliate because your subject joined the enemy's slaves. If you think you can destroy his leadership by direct attack, try and make it work. But do not be too zealous with the challenges and chaos. When those who are in allegiance to our enemy are pushed to declare their dependence on him this opens the door for a deeper knowledge of who the enemy is. You can be assured when this happens our enemy will respond to this desire. The physical is often the open door to the spiritual for these vermin. Our goal for our subjects is not a greater awareness of their frailty and need that could in any way open them to influence from our enemy. There must be wrong beliefs or doubts that you set up in advance before you can take any ground back through pain or suffering.

Later on, I will help you to know how to use him for much greater damage. A religious fool is our greatest opportunity to mock the enemy before the world. However, you have much learning to do. Begin at once to cut him off from any friendships and groups that he was involved with before his betrayal of Our Founder Below. Make him feel the pain of being different, an outsider who doesn't fit in. A good dose of mocking and ridicule will quickly harden him up.

Your advising friend,
Wyrmwud

P. S. Lest you think our enemy is simple minded, remember he is no push over. He has yielded control of his kingdom in ways that we cannot dream of. We cannot conceive of why he has given such liberty, but we believe he will soon reveal his true plan to control and dominate the universe. Our filthosophers have just not figured out how.

From: <Wyrmwud> wyrmwud@hell.edu
To: <Tweazel> tweazel@hell.edu
Subject: <u>Religion is for the old</u>

Tweazel,

I can see evidence of your hard work to contain the damage of your subject's turning to the enemy. If I had not seen that, you can be assured I would have removed your disgusting presence from the fraternity. Do not let up.

Because of your complete lack of communication with me it is now too late to get your subject to write off religion. Since he has turned on us, it seems you have done the next best thing and pushed him into a small church where the old man attends. I have read the records and there are not many young people there. But beware, the enemy is reported to be there.

Exploit any contact he has with religion and convince him it is only for ancient, boring human vermin who don't have anything better to do. Point out the outdated suits the old buzzards wear. Emphasize the greased back hair, wrinkles and old black-framed glasses all around him. Highlight the old lady sleeping through the service with drool falling from her lip. Show him the women with hair up in a bun, wearing dresses that look like they were made from curtains. Convince him that is what the enemy considers sexy. Tell him that his future wife will end up looking like that. Let him think that church is only for human slime who need a crutch to get through life. The feelings from the experience he had with the enemy will wear off. How quickly it does we cannot determine as it is dependent on the vermin and how much they understand about the enemy. (See my previous notes on the enemy's influence over the vermin. The notes I wrote to stop this from happening, I will add.)

Like a drug, the experience will wear off and he will need more contact with the enemy in order to keep on. You must work to convince him that as the experience wears off, there was nothing more to it. Once the feeling is gone you must make him believe the enemy is gone too.

You have not worked hard enough in his family. You must convince family members that they know the *real* him and this is only a stage he is going through. Stage a fight with his brother or sister in an area you know he is weak in. He will still have all his old habits and reactions. His brother or sister will know how to push his buttons, so get them to provoke him just so that they can see that their *real* brother is still there. Since his reactions are still there, he is the same. This will allow them to write off the enemy as some sort of social thing that only weak vermin need.

Begin to do some research on the local colleges. We have a lot of influence there and it would give us a chance to mock his religious beliefs. It would open up the doors to many of the vermin his age who are on our side. Put the thought in his head that if many of the human slime his age don't believe in the enemy, maybe they are right. Suggest that the majority knows what is right.

Your alert friend,
Wyrmwud

From: <Wyrmwud> wyrmwud@hell.edu
To: <Tweazel> tweazel@hell.edu
Subject: <u>College</u>

Tweazel,

You have helped your subject to settle into the vermin's weekly meetings with the enemy. He has become familiar with the language and how things are done. Work hard at helping him use the old man's language to talk about the enemy. I trust the old buzzard still uses all the 'thee' and 'thou' words from centuries ago. Have the old vermin scold him harshly when he uses street slang or modern words. At the very least have them not be able to understand much of what he says. Try and create the feeling within him that he has all the problems and must change everything and not the old folks. If he begins to use their language and adapt to them it will create a gap if he talks about it with his friends at school. They will immediately shut him down.

Have them keep asking him when he is going to do something with his life and go into 'ministry.' Help your subject realize the most cherished and loved among the human scum are those involved in ministry full time. I will explain why later.

College seems to be going OK. I notice you have not been able to entice him to any parties or to hang out with those we have a strong influence with. This is not a good sign for a first year student. He should be wanting to fit in and feeling the pressure of not doing what everyone else is doing. I don't like it.

I don't care if he likes software programming, computers or technology. He may be good at it but we have to think about how we can use it for our purposes. It is just a tool. It is the use of the tool we must be concerned about. Thankfully few people in his church know much about computers and some are even terrified of them. Because of this you have done a good job making your subject believe that the enemy doesn't like technology. This will only help him believe the enemy is even more ancient than the people in the meetings he attends. Excellent! We know your subject can't really care about someone he pictures as old-fashioned and out of touch with the world he lives in.

Your educated friend,
Wyrmwud

From: <Wyrmwud> wyrmwud@hell.edu
To: <Tweazel> tweazel@hell.edu
Subject: New opportunity

Tweazel,

One year of school was enough. I didn't like
how he was doing and we don't want too
many educated people in the enemy's camp. I
see that he has decided to start his own business with software and computer technology. I
know you wrote of pushing him into this but I
doubt you had much to say about it. Perhaps I
have underestimated you. You might not be
hopeless after all. Time will tell but you can
rest assured, I will not let my guard down. As
you know, the business world is where we
have secured our strongest hold and thus will
be able to have much influence over him.

A new business is a birthing process. It will
provide the opportunity to charge him with
hope and misdirect all of his energy in busyness. He should be able to forget about the old
man from the youth organization. As there will
be more distractions and challenges than he
will know what to do with, use all this to limit
any conversation he has with the enemy. When
he sits to rest, fill his mind with all the things
he must do.

Because of our work done centuries ago, your
subject's association with the church and its

emphasis on ministry, I will assume that he feels like owning a business is somehow a second-class profession. There will be a sense or desire in his heart to want to please our enemy. We have convinced the human scum that this can only be done through full-time religious work. As business is not considered religious work, he will feel guilty and con-demned for this apparent show of disrespect. (Do not take the hard work of centuries lightly. This little revelation took much planning and years of distortion to make it so strongly ac-cepted and common today.)

Keep this feeling of shame and guilt alive, just under the surface. The more he succeeds in his business the dirtier he will feel. Each time he talks with the enemy, stir up these feelings. Don't let him consciously talk about them with the enemy as you don't want it exposed to the light. He should assume that the enemy is pleased only with full-time religious work and thus he will not want to bring it up in his conversation with him.

Work hard on his desire for power. This is obviously a key reason why he wanted to start his own business. Our filthosophers tell us the desire for power was placed there by the en-emy. You must misdirect it. The enemy unfairly declares he has all power and waits for your subject to recognize his need for it and go to him to get it. You must push to meet that need in your subject through money. Convince him that money will be the means of attaining power. When this happens he won't seek out power from the enemy's nauseating spirit. Let me say this clearly, money will replace that disgusting spirit. He will look to money to be the source of his power for what he wants to do. If this happens you have him because he will then serve money and not the enemy.

Your pleased friend,
Wyrmwud

From: <Wyrmwud> wyrmwud@hell.edu
To: <Tweazel> tweazel@hell.edu
Subject: <u>Success</u>

Tweazel,

Your subject is doing well with his business.
The software program he wrote is in great
demand and he has more opportunities then he
knows what to do with. If you work it right
this success has the power to wonderfully
corrupt your subject like no failure can. You are
lucky your report and surveillance was in
agreement about his success. Know that you
are being watched and cannot make a mistake.
Internal affairs had us completely checked out.
They are very serious about an enemy's slave
in leadership and check out any leader who
appears to be succeeding. They are keeping a
file on us, so beware. They will also gather any
dirt they can find on your subject, in case you
need it.

Their report stated that because of your use of
your subject's success and its positive effect on
him, he is rated as lukewarm. Because of this
rating we were not reprimanded. If he was in
any other area, then I would be deeply concerned but you have allowed him to succeed in
business and we can use much of that for our
advantage. There are very few businessmen
who understand their place in the enemy's
work. I am pleased you have limited his in-

volvement in the enemy's camp to giving. Make sure he feels guilty for giving as he is giving some of the 'dirty' money he has made from his second-class profession. Even the good he thinks he is doing brings with it a condemnation that will keep him ineffective.

Introduce him to other men and women his age who are successful. He will desire to fit in with them. Make sure they are typical business vermin who measure success by material standards. Open his eyes to the world of name brands. Let him accept the lie that unless he is wearing the right clothes by the right design-ers, he will not be accepted. If he truly wants to be accepted by others in this group then he will want to show them his success and this will open the door for him to spend lots of money on himself. As I have checked in records, there are other business owners who seem to be closely watched and have no areas that concern us. Be sure and talk with Zitcore and Arrowgance as you may be able to help each other out.

You were sloppy in allowing your subject to hire the enemy's slaves but I can see that it worked out to your advantage. I will assume you checked them out completely and knew that they only spoke the language of the enemy's camp and nothing more. Your subject quickly realized that often those who say they are in the enemy's camp arrive to work late, don't get their work done on time and even when it is finally completed, it is done so poorly that it has to be redone by someone else. They assume because they are in the enemy's camp and their boss is in the enemy's camp that they don't have to work too hard. Generalize this understanding so that soon your subject will think that all of the enemy's slaves will have the same problem and your subject will want to distance himself from hiring them or even associating with them. This will further distance him from the enemy and any influence he may have over him.

Bring superficial friends around your subject who will want to enjoy his new-found wealth. Place them like leeches around him to suck his soul dry. There are many we have influence over who will want to hang out with him because he is successful.

Have them speak highly of all his talents and strengths and the great job he has done to 'earn' his success. Have them use that word 'earn' at every opportunity they can. Another key word is 'deserve.' You cannot overuse these words. He will begin to believe some of the things they say about him even though he knows they are not true. Yet, he wants to believe them, so in the end he will.

Your investigated friend,
Wyrmwud

From: \<Wyrmwud\> wyrmwud@hell.edu
To: \<Tweazel\> tweazel@hell.edu
Subject: <u>Death</u>

Tweazel,

Or should I call you weasel instead? Other
names come to mind like: idiot, fool, maggot. I
trust you have the discernment to realize I am
upset. You described your subject as disturbed
and confused. The death of the old man who
was in charge of the youth organization has
stirred him up. You wrote of your subject
standing over the casket, staring at his old
friend. You mocked his tears as if they were
meaningless and told you nothing about your
subject. Then you stated it was your desire to
use this to your advantage. You are pushing
your subject to ponder death!?! I could not
believe it when I read it. It is unthinkable that
you wanted him to ponder death. Like a child
with his first taste of sugar, you have tasted of
his fear and you want more. And like a child
who eats too much sugar, your incompetence
could make you very sick.

I checked with Smear, the old man's guardian,
just before Smear's boss came to deal with him.
Smear was with his subject until just before the
end. All of the fraternity had been called off
and normal rules of passage applied. What
your subject could not see was the enemy
coming to take the man away. Thankfully the

human vermin can only see within the confines of the physical world. Smear turned away and did not watch as in accordance with the rules. Ever since the hated one died, Our Founder Below changed the rules and deals very seriously with anyone who watches the enemy come to take those on his side to be with him. It is said to be hideous beyond words and if seen, burns into your memory pictures that will torment you all your life. I only wish you could have seen the look on Smear's face when he knew his boss was coming to him to deal with his inability to turn one of his subjects to our side. It is a look you will become familiar with if you don't get your work done.

Let me be clear about this. Do not allow your subject to focus on death. There is a deeper mystery here that we do not understand. We are spirits who will never die. The human scum know they will die and they have no experience for what is on the other side. Everything in the physical world that they care about, are comfortable with and use to define themselves by is stripped away in a joyfully terrifying moment called death.

Those in the enemy's camp hope there is more but we try and convince them it is a blind hope. If you lead him to ponder death he will only find his own mortality. It is one time where they are directly confronted with reality and all their illusions are susceptible to collapse. Your subject will think of other parasites he genuinely cares about and what he wants most out of life. All his material successes and the illusions you have attached to them might collapse. Reality is not something we want him to focus on.

I had one subject who was a chief executive, a leader of leaders. When he watched a family member die I stared in horror as the enemy appeared and tried to seduce him with supposed comfort and compassion. In the midst of the blinding light I could almost hear the lies to this subject. From our research on the enemy, I am sure they sounded something like: *Is all this busyness worth it? What's really important in life? A conversation with friends over a cup of coffee? A long walk enjoying the beauty all around? Joyous laughter playing with your children?* It was only with some last minute emergencies from a friend in need and distractions the subject gladly accepted to avoid the pain he felt, that I was able to convince him to put off thinking about these thoughts until later which, by the way, has never happened. My subject teetered on the very edge of seeing that work for work's sake was futile. This idea could not be allowed to grow in his thick skull.

In dealing with death you must be very careful — something it seems you are incapable of. Nevertheless I will hold your sorry little hand and tell you why to be careful.

• We do not want your subject to realize that work for work's sake is empty. The less his pathetic little heart is connected to what he does the more he learns to embrace a mundane useless life. With this acceptance comes a sinking understanding that he is not important and he has nothing to give the world.

• We do not want your subject to understand that he does not have the power to get what he truly wants or needs. Feed him lies about how technology, or money, or relationships with girls or sports can satisfy him. It doesn't matter, as long as he believes that what he wants is somewhere in his material world and all he has to do is find it.

• Once you have misdirected him to accept his place in mundane work, you can then help him see that life is cheap and can be squandered with no great losses involved. He must not see that the enemy considers his life precious, something that must be guarded and cherished. Death can remind him of the mystery of life and this idea must be expelled.

• The last point is that he must never be allowed to dwell on the fact that he can't take anything with him. All that he has, a house, clothes, computers or technology, cars, sports equipment, ect. - none of it can go with him. The blind little vermin have no idea how hard we push to make it a wonderful distraction.

<u>Whatever you do, don't let him see that only a fool would work his whole life for material things he must give up when he dies.</u> These human vermin do not want to see themselves as fools and will often take the first distraction you offer to protect themselves from this revelation.

A human parasite in the enemy's camp, who is doing what he loves to do, is our worst nightmare. I know you have yet to see a subject who admits he needs help and invites others to join him, or one that sees life as a gift with its most precious moments having little to do with the material world, but when you do you will never forget the power they exude and agony they can cause you. The influence they have is unbearable. You can even smell their presence as they are so vile. Seeing death awakens in the human vermin these desires and you must guard against that.

This could be a huge loss to all your hard work. I am sure the enemy's presence was so bright during this time that you have lost your voice to your subject for a season. As a result of this he will have a much better understanding of the world he lives in and who he is as a slave of the enemy. He will be on guard. If what you have written is as bad as it sounds then I am sure by now your subject is firmly reestablished in the enemy's camp.

Fight as if your very life depended on it. For it does.

Your angry advisor,
Wyrmwud

From: <Wyrmwud> wyrmwud@hell.edu
To: <Tweazel> tweazel@hell.edu
Subject: <u>Insecurity</u>

Tweazel,

I am still furious at the thought of your stupidity and lack of communication. Knowing how much trouble you can cause, I thought I better email quickly to make sure you don't do anything worse. The best attack to use during times of change is to find and feed the insecurity that is there. I can see you haven't recognized the symptoms of it in your subject's confusion and discomfort. Are you blind? Open your eyes. In the West where they have luxuries beyond other nations' dreams, the vermin have become obsessed with themselves — thanks to our help. We have made them self-conscious about who they are and linked their identity to what they possess. Thus their focus is on security. This puts their attention on power and control with a desire to deal with any threat. As security is something that you can never have enough of they are like a dog chasing its tail.

What must matter to you is that your subject is insecure and that is an open door for us. Insecurity means that for a brief moment, he has realized that he doesn't understand who he is or he doesn't have the power to protect himself. Our researchers have realized this as a ploy of the enemy to open up his slaves to further his domination and control in their lives. He is often shaking anything that can be shaken in their temporal world so they do not put their trust in it. If they cling to their relationships, money, power, food or even knowledge, he is there to make them see it cannot be their life. He seems to highly value that they trust him and him alone. This shaking process is our bread and butter as your subject will not recognize that it is the enemy trying to get his attention and will usually turn his eyes inward or just take action to do something to distract himself.

I am embarrassed to have to write what every good fraternity member should know by heart. But I am reminded of your grades from Deceiver's School and that you barely passed. When I took you on, I thought that maybe your poor showing was just because you didn't like the instructors who I know can be harsh. But I fear it is your own stupidity and now I am associated with you so I must walk you through things if you are ever going to make anything of yourself. Listen up as I will try and do what I am sure no other fraternity member would do and that is to make the obvious, obvious even to an imbecile.

Now, in regards to your subject, there are two basic ways to get him to respond to insecurity in his leadership.

The first reaction of the human vermin when they are insecure is that they will want to take control. They will feel threatened in some way and you must push them to respond in a dominating, overpowering way that makes it clear to everyone involved whose will is being done. Have your subject use harsh words, anger, telling everyone exactly what they should do, making sure everything is being done according to his preferences. Promote all of these elements of control. The key behind this is that he must instill fear and those under him must know who has the authority and thus the power. It is his and his alone.

The second reaction is where they abdicate their responsibility. Some of the human vermin appear weaker and don't like confrontation. They pretend they don't want to hurt others and so they hide and thus let anybody do anything they want. It is a free for all with everyone involved. The most important point here is to cut off all communication and have your subject pretend he is not aware of what is going on.

Push him towards domination or abdication when he is insecure. These "buttons" seem to lie in the heart of every leader and it is up to you to push them to our benefit. You can destroy much of his influence this way.

As I am writing I realize you may not even understand the role identity plays in our work. Although it was covered at Deceiver's School, I can see that you didn't get it as you seemed to have been given a free ride through the system. The key points are as follows:

• The enemy has chosen to use identity to define your subject's value and meaning. The human vermin seem to have some sort of link with the enemy. For reasons we have not fully understood, our enemy breathed his breath into them instead of speaking them into existence like he did with the rest of creation. Our researchers and filthosophers suggest that this means that they are the unfinished breath of our enemy. Just as a breath is a word waiting for release, so they are to finish our enemy's breath in them by their words and choices.

• We do not know how we were created, obviously because we weren't there to see what he did. We do know that he made us to be dominated by him and to be his slaves but we broke free from his authoritarian control. He is the only one who knows this creative process but we are confident that with time we will understand the importance of his breath in them. For now, all you need to understand is that it created a link in them to long for an identity that is bigger than their own. This longing is what creates the insecurity that we want to turn against them. Your subject realizes he is not content with who he is and he desires more. . .we don't know what more is. But that is not important as neither does your subject. What we want to do is bend or twist his identity so that it will open the door for us.

• Identity involves how others see him. I wrote earlier of our attack against the enemy and tried to spell out clearly how we must destroy his influence over his creation by distorting their perception of his nature and character. Let me say it another way to make sure your little pea-brain can understand. We are trying to destroy his identity. His or any leader's perceived identity is what gives them influence over those who follow them.

• Identity involves how your subject sees himself. How he sees himself will determine his confidence and willingness to take risks. We heard the hated one say, "Love your neighbor as yourself." This opened the door to understanding for our researchers that the human vermin's capacity to relate to others is tied to how they view themselves. Although we have clearly debunked the myth of love, the concept is important for us. The key for your work is that your subject's capacity to destroy others is determined by his capacity to fixate on or hate himself. You must destroy how he sees himself. You seem to be aware of this and thus your attempt to bring shame on him earlier in his life.

• Identity forms the basis of how the human vermin organize themselves and relate to each other. Like a chess game, once each figure is identified, their moves, power and placement is established. The more bent and misunderstood their identity is, the harder it is for them to organize themselves. True chaos is the result of a complete loss of or having a distorted or wrong identity.

I fear I have given you more than your pea-brain can handle for now. Just remember, his identity is like the hub of a bicycle wheel. It holds all the spokes together and allows the wheel to move. Twist his identity and you ruin him. Insecurity is your chance to bust the wheel. Use it to your advantage.

Your cautious friend,
Wyrmwud

From: <Wyrmwud> wyrmwud@hell.edu
To: <Tweazel> tweazel@hell.edu
Subject: Stability

Tweazel,

I am very disappointed to hear of your
subject's continued success. It has reached the
point where it becomes a concern to us because
of the influence he now has over hundreds of
people. He has not destroyed himself with his
success, and has even lost much of his lust for
proving his success to others. We are going to
have to work harder and use all of our re-
sources if we are going to still use his leadership to benefit our side. This will require much
greater understanding of the fraternity's work
and I trust you have done your homework
recently so that you can try to manipulate your
subject as he rises in influence.

For many centuries we were able to implant
deeply in their understanding the myth of
stability. Because change was so slow and
subtle, we were able to bend their natural
desire for stability into an expectation that all
life was and should be stable. Another way of
saying it is that we wanted them to think that
life was like a long, straight and flat road. This
has come in very handy as any hill or twist in
the road, any form of speeding change, is now
seen as a problem that must be fixed. A foe that
must be fought. They think that something is

wrong if the way is not flat, stable and straight. Living in the midst of constantly twisting roads with large mountains to cross, or constant change, brings insecurity and that opens the door for us and our plans. The myth of stability has been put in place in earlier centuries, just for the times we have entered now. This is where the battle will be won or lost. Billions of souls can be ours as there are more of these 'living foods' alive now than any other time in the history of man. Many years of strategy and preparation has gone into preparing them for how they view the world now. Use it for your advantage.

Your vigilant friend,
Wyrmwud

From: <Wyrmwud> wyrmwud@hell.edu
To: <Tweazel> tweazel@hell.edu
Subject: <u>History</u>

Tweazel,

I am glad you had the respect to ask. I would have been ready to consume you if you had moved ahead without understanding what I meant by our having an advantage. You can rest assured I would have seen your ignorance. If you don't know what I want, ask, because by now it should be clear that what I want, is what you must want if you are to succeed.

As you have forgotten history, as well as everything else, I will have to write a rather brief reminder of our previous work that you may use the effects of it today. During what the human slime called medieval times, science was a very different tool than it is today. During this time it was based on faith and reason and its main goal was to understand the meaning and significance of things the enemy created. Up until this time it was very natural for the human vermin to see themselves as a part of their world. They were linked to creation and responsible for its oversight.

I do trust you are following what I am saying for this wearies me to have to be so simple and explain everything to you. We began a very subtle attack during this time that your subject would call the Enlightenment. As the human scum began to realize that the Earth was not the center of the universe in a geographic sense, although we twisted it to seem like it was in every other sense, it began to shake them up.

Descartes began to study the world and created a way of thinking that was a real help to us. He separated the mind and body. Or another way of saying it, is the separation of spirit and the physical world. The spiritual was important to him (we removed that emphasis later) but it wasn't needed to understand the material world in his thinking and research as a scientist. As far as Descartes was concerned, the material world was a machine and nothing but a machine. This basic spark of an idea was flamed by our most gifted filthosophers into a fully burning philosophy. Science could be seen as a purely objective realm in the study of the natural world. The human scum became convinced that they could be objective observers free of any values or relationship to what was studied. Their spirits played no part in the 'real' world.

In case you are not making the connections, this small spark of an idea of separating the material world from the spiritual world, eventually became the understanding of what your subject — I hope he has no conscious idea of this but that would be too good to be true —

today would call the secular and the sacred. The sacred is the spiritual world with religion. The secular is the physical world and other areas linked to it like business, government, arts. etc.

Let me explain how we have turned this to our advantage on a large scale. Look at the continent of Africa. The enemy has been sending workers there for hundreds of years. The enemy's slaves talk over and over again about how many are on the enemy's side there. Yet look at the poverty, disease, violence and corruption. It is as wonderfully bad or worse now than ever. Their message has only been concerned with the vermin's spirit. Because of the separation of the spirit and matter, they have done little to help the Africans in other areas because we have convinced them that it does not matter. They have won new slaves for the enemy's camp, but we have influenced millions in just the opposite way. Because those that saw this mess are focused only on the material world, they believe that if the message of the enemy's slaves doesn't help in the material world, why should they believe?

We have discredited the work of the enemy and many are looking to us for answers. All because his slaves think their job is finished once the vermin's spirit is joined to the enemy's side. This is not limited to Africa. It is the same in many of the cities in the developed world. The cities where many of the enemy's slaves live are socially no better off than other cities where there are not many of the enemy's slaves. We have convinced millions that the enemy's message doesn't have to make a difference in real life. This is all because of the separation between spirit and matter. We have been able to mock the hated one's statement that his slaves are the salt of the earth.

If you have not heard it said before you must remember that ideas have consequences. The modern luxury that you take for granted today in the separation of the secular and sacred was just an idea in the mind of a scientist and philosopher hundreds of years ago. Ideas carry within them the seeds of the future for the world in which the enemy operates and the territory over which we fight. A victory for us in the next century is often dependent on the ideas we work with in the minds of the leaders today.

This exhausts me too much to continue. I have other work to do. Ponder these thoughts and I will write more later.

Your weary friend,
Wyrmwud

From: <Wyrmwud> wyrmwud@hell.edu
To: <Tweazel> tweazel@hell.edu
Subject: <u>History continued</u>

Tweazel,

Just when I think you couldn't do anything
more stupid, I get a note from the Deceiver's
School. You informed them I said they were
harsh on you. You also stated that I said it was
their fault you didn't learn. I have met with
them personally and the matter has been
cleared up. I have agreed to send them all my
notes on my instruction with you that they
may use them at the school. Tweazel, you are
too young and powerless to even think you
could knock me off my spot. Do not try it
again. I will not be so kind next time.

Your apparent disdain for the philosophical
and historical side is of great curiosity to me.
You seem to assume that you will have great
influence in your subject without understanding the bigger picture which you are operating
from and trying to influence him to think and
work towards. He has easily defended himself
from your childish attempts of hidden plea-
sures with prostitutes, he is not consumed with
spending his money on himself, he meets
weekly with other slaves of the enemy, he even
gives some of his filthy money to the church.
Your little bag of tempter's tricks has run out.
If you do not understand the historical frame-

work, you will always be the little peon you are today and will never rise to any true status or have any real power. You seem to have caught little of the consequences of what I wrote so I must continue the agony of spelling everything out for you.

Somehow in your small thoughts, you seem to think I was saying that we created the logic and reasoning that Descartes used. You hinted that you wanted to put these together and at work in your subject. Listen and listen clearly, we cannot create anything. Our enemy has been the only one to truly create anything, although our scientists are madly at work to learn how to do this too. Our enemy created logic and reasoning as all other aspects of creation. We are only bending it to our purpose. Logic and reasoning will lead the vermin to our enemy if there is no twisting, pain or selfishness involved. Something you can be grateful there is plenty of in our subjects. Before I go any further, let me continue on with your history lesson. It would pay you to listen attentively.

As I was saying earlier, the philosophy that was birthed through Descartes' ideas was based on his separation of the material world from the spiritual world. He then went on to form a way of thinking for the analysis of the material world. He had great faith in scientific knowledge as the way to understand his world. Simply put, his way of analyzing the world around him was to break up all thought and problems into pieces and then to arrange the pieces in their logical order. With the help of other scientists like Newton, it was discovered that nature worked according to strict laws. They thought everything in the material world could be explained in terms of the logical arrangement and movement of its parts. Or another way of saying it is that the cause determines the effect. You can explain any effect if you can isolate the cause.

As we began to work with these ideas, we were able to rid many of their minds of any reference to the spirit and thus our enemy. We convinced them that they were the masters of their own fate and if they could only determine the laws that caused the movement of everything in the material world, then they could determine the outcome. Like a car that a person knows how to operate and thus uses for his or her purposes, so all of life, once understood, could be used by them. Life was predictable and could be controlled. All that was needed was a complete knowledge of these laws of cause and effect. They could become, once this knowledge was gathered, like a god, able to predict and control all the material universe by their understanding and will. All in the name of science.

As I mentioned earlier, this capacity to observe and study their world is not automatically evil and thus to our benefit. The human scum have been able to remove some of our most wonderful and hideous diseases, as well as ease some of their struggles and agony through the use of this reasoning and thinking process. Medicine, communication and agriculture have all grown far more productive.

If we had known of the good that would come out of all of this we might not have so willingly tried to push the little vermin in this direction. Our enemy has brought much good out of it so you must not get too proud in thinking we have been the only one at work in this direction. It seems he has used this for his good as well. But let me end on a positive note. We have also seen the development of atomic bombs, chemical warfare and machinery that could cause mass destruction. This has brought great hope to our side.

Your friend who grows weary explaining everything to a complete moron,
Wyrmwud

From: <Wyrmwud> wyrmwud@hell.edu
To: <Tweazel> tweazel@hell.edu
Subject: <u>Machines and your subject's thinking</u>

Tweazel,

I have not heard much from you recently and I hope it is because you are busy studying my notes and there is not much happening with your subject. The last time you did not keep me posted it meant there was trouble. I will check my other contacts to make sure you are on task and that this is not the case.

A key point to remember: we helped develop (from Descartes) the Cartesian philosophy, research and thinking process where everything is broken down into pieces. These parts are then analyzed on their own so that all the elements can be understood individually. In other words, all aspects of any complex phenomena can be understood by reducing it into its pieces. There is no great whole, each part can be understood on its own. This thinking helped fuel the now-assumed reality that the material world is a machine.

As I know the above thoughts may have been over your little putz of a brain, I will spell out the potential benefits to you. Your subject will only see things in fragments and when he wants to understand something he will isolate the parts and think only about them. Tied with this is that there is no spirit, the material world is all there is and it works like a machine. This feeds into the human vermin's craving for power, control and prediction that they can use to dominate their world.

As far as your subject goes and the rest of those in the enemy's camp, most will be thinking that a vast and complex machine has been entrusted into their care. Like a clock maker who created a clock and then stepped back, the vermin think the enemy made the material world and then has stepped aside. He was infinitely rational, his works were totally predictable and a few simple laws would reveal how everything worked.

As you have proven to be far inferior to my mind, let me simplify this point for you to fully capture what I mean before I move on. There are two key points you must remember. First, the human vermin will organize around the understanding of a machine. Second, because of this, they will break everything down into parts, not thinking about the big picture or the relationship among the parts. These are very important pieces for you to understand as you work with your subject.

Why this is important I will explain later, but for now it is a way that your subject can fulfill his desire to be in complete control over those who follow him. Describing his organization as a machine is a wonderful way for your subject to limit his thinking. This mentality of a machine is so strong that it is the only way he will think about his organization. It is a part of his cultural understanding and thus without thinking about it your subject will blindly interpret it to be a model that the enemy uses.

Your rational friend,
Wyrmwud

From: \<Wyrmwud> wyrmwud@hell.edu
To: \<Tweazel> tweazel@hell.edu
Subject: <u>Enemy's plans</u>

Tweazel,

I see somehow I have not been clear enough.
You still think that this has little to do with
your tempting and influencing your subject
today. I must remind myself that you are an
idiot who cannot see past the instant pleasure
you can get through your subject's fear and
pain. Bear in mind that our focus is on leaders
and how they work through their followers.

Years ago when the hated one joined the vermin and actually lived in their midst (the
cheater has an unfair advantage knowing what
it is like to have a body), he gave us clues as to
his purpose and how he wanted to help them.
As you are aware, once a word is spoken it
exists for all time for those who can dial into its
frequency. We have captured the words of the
hated one and our best filthosophers have
analyzed them trying to figure out the hidden
meaning in them. They have listened to the
messages thousands of times and although
most of the meanings are still not clear there
are some things we think we understand.

Through careful analyzation it was realized
that one of the primary purposes and plans he
had for them was built on how they worked

together. (This thought is still under investigation as it seems too simple and it is believed there was a hidden message in it.) He went as far as to say out loud that our enemy wanted his servants to be one as our enemy is one. What an arrogant, ridiculous idea that he is the standard for how they live. Remember our missions statement.

Later, one of his slaves wrote on the enemy's behalf, that all the human vermin would know about the enemy by his slaves' capacity to relate to each other. As difficult as it is to believe, it seems our sworn enemy actually wants them to organize themselves and work together in some form of unity.

I must stop and take a deep breath here for having to actually write these things out is wearying beyond words. Trying to think like the enemy and spell things out so you can understand his strategy and the focus of our work is exhausting for me and I quickly feel drained.

I trust you are beginning to understand all my preparation up to this point about why the philosophy they use in organizing themselves and working together is so important. Our enemy wants them to work together and says in fact that they will only have his blessing and power if they do work together. How they think about organizing themselves will determine how much blessing and power the enemy will give them. Our strategy has thus been to attack their ideas about what it means to work together so that they will not have the blessing of our enemy and this will open the door for us to enter into their world.

How they think the enemy organizes the world will be the same way they organize it.

Your shrewd friend,
Wyrmwud

From: \<Wyrmwud\> wyrmwud@hell.edu
To: \<Tweazel\> tweazel@hell.edu
Subject: <u>Modern organization</u>

Tweazel,

I am at a loss to believe that you cannot even think of the characteristics of a machine and how it relates to an organization. Your subject's continued success and business growth means that he will be struggling with how to organize everyone. When he started the business they all knew each other and did what they had to do. They could just talk with each other whenever they had a question. It was very informal. Now there are too many of the vermin and he will have to think about structure. This is your opportunity, idiot! Use it to your advantage. I know you don't know how to use it for your advantage. I can almost hear you whining and complaining that my wisdom is too much for you. So I will spell it out for you. You must create systems that slowly, day by aching day, grind down and destroy those who work in them.

One system we have been successfully infiltrating is education. Many years ago we recognized the importance of leadership in this area and made this a focus of much of our energy. Destroying young children has such delightful long-term effects. Anyway, before I get carried away on the joy of crushing the spirit in the vermin's children and this then becomes the only thing you remember, I best keep to our discussion. A school is an organization that is run like a machine. Here is how.

• Teachers in a school system [machine] are trained to do their task and only their task. If there is a problem or they wear out you quickly replace them with another teacher [part] who can take their place. One teacher is like all other teachers. There is nothing special about teachers, they can be made like any other part in the system, when they are needed.

• Each teacher is taught to do the same thing over and over and over. Teachers are given the illusion of freedom in the system by being able to organize their classes as they want. They can change their bulletin board or even the order of the subjects taught. But let them change the content of the curriculum in any way and the system [machine] will crush them. In the end, even the most creative vermin will teach only what the system allows them to teach.

• The way a school works is through standardization. Children are the material the system works on. Children all enter in at the same time of year and at the same age. Once the children are in the system each child is run through the same process. There is no allowance for creativity or difference. They all study the same material to pass the same test to know the same answers to the same pre-established questions. Once they are through the system they are all expected to be the same output.

• If there is a problem with the system it can be fixed by analyzing where and what the problem is, and using the right tools to fix it. Feelings and values don't play a part, they just muddy the waters. Deal with the objective facts and you can fix any problem.

Since I have known you for a while, and given you so much of my precious time, I know you will not see clearly how the educational system is like a machine. Or, how important the model of a machine is in causing them pain. So let me spell out what a machine is like so that you might see the connection between the model they use and how it becomes a framework for how they organize themselves. Look for how the educational system described above is similar to the machine described below.

• A machine is made up of parts. If a part breaks or wears out you just replace it. There are many different parts in stock to replace a part that goes bad. A part is just raw material that is made in a certain way. There is nothing special about it.

• A machine is made to do the same thing over and over and over. There is no freedom within the parts to do anything else but the exact task it is built to do. There is no adaptation. The more specialization for the parts the better. A machine needs to work in a stable environment.

• A machine works through standardization. You have an input that is pre-established. All material being used by the machine must be standardized. Once the material is in the machine, it goes through the exact same process with a known output. If there is variation in the output, something is wrong with the machine.

• The machine is not alive, it exists to serve a pre-established function. If it ceases to serve that function it can be removed and thrown away or used for parts somewhere else.

• If there is a problem, you analyze what is wrong and fix it. All problems can be fixed and taken care of. You give mechanics tools to take care of machines.

Do you see the connection?

I trust now you can see the importance of influencing how they think about organizing themselves. Let me say it clearly, the reason we can cause the pain we do is because they have organized themselves with the machine as a model. There are teachers who genuinely care for the students but we identify them quickly and grind and crush them into conformity before they can do too much damage. The machine is designed to work on teachers just as well as it works on students.

I trust you now see the obvious, untold pain and damage that has been done to some of the young vermin because they didn't fit into the system [machine]. If they had trouble learning, we helped them to see that it is obviously the "material" the machine is working with, themselves.

No one ever questions the machine. The students end up feeling like they are dumb, they can't learn, they will never be smart enough. Many of the students carry these feelings with them for their whole life and it is like an open wound within them. If you want a response then you can push against the laceration and cause them pain whenever you like. This is a delicious way to warp and distort their understanding of their identity. Look into your subject and I can almost guarantee that there will be some pain within him from school.

Your smart friend,
Wyrmwud

From: <Wyrmwud> wyrmwud@hell.edu
To: <Tweazel> tweazel@hell.edu
Subject: <u>Enemy's laws</u>

Tweazel,

I told you, you would find more pain in your subject if you had the brains to know where to look. His disgust for the term 'learning' is a real benefit and help to us. It seems well worth your time spent to find out that on one of his tests when he was younger he was rated "borderline mentally retarded." Don't ever let him think it was the teacher's inability to challenge him or that he had a different learning style. Instead tie it to his identity. Convince him that he is a moron who can't learn. Once he accepts this wonderful revelation from us, no one else will be able to convince him otherwise. Sometimes, when this happens, you can even get a subject to spend his whole life running from this fear, trying to prove he is not stupid.
A more subtle use of this is to put him in places where there are mentally retarded people and bring on the shame he feels. Watch him squirm and get out of there as fast as he can.

I have picked up in your last notes that you seem to expend great effort in belittling our enemy. I like the attitude, but you act as if the enemy is not all-powerful. Let me state quickly and strongly that you must be very careful with this strategy. We are forced to admit that he is all-powerful and could squash us with his little finger in a second if he wanted to. You cannot fight with him like that. Our battle and, our contention with the enemy is that power is not the primary basis for leadership. Thus, our war is a moral war and we are fighting for all of creation's freedom. Wisdom and cunning are vitally important for this freedom and Our Exalted Founder Below is wise enough to lead us. Our declaration is that the enemy is selfish and just because he is all-powerful, he uses his power to oppress his creation. We must do everything we can to stop him. Remember our mission statement.

If you are to truly be effective in breaking down his work you must study the enemy's ways and principles. I know this sounds crazy but you must know his law as well as he does. When you know how he works, you can understand his strategy and how to attack him. It has allowed Our Exalted Founder Below to bring us as far as we have come. He was able to use the law against our enemy and keep us safe. Let me give you an example of understanding our enemy's strategy so that you can see how we have countered his intent.

Our enemy wants the vermin to obey from their hearts. It is in line with his declared desire to have a relationship with them. (Excuse me while I throw up at just the thought of this.) He declares this as his highest priority. But the human scum joined our side and their hearts became wonderfully bent. With this strategy we helped them quickly forget the rules he had placed in their hearts. He intervened and gave the human vermin ten oppressive laws in order to help them know what he wanted. He couldn't stand the thought of the human vermin enjoying their freedom and the parties they were having with us. Our filthosophers studied his strategy in giving these laws and believed it was his desire to show his slaves how he made them and what they needed to do to be happy. With this in mind we immediately set up a counter attack. Remember, we must know what he is doing in order to use it to our advantage. Don't fight the fact that there are commandments, just misdirect them.

The vermin had the desire given to them by the enemy, to do what was right and he made it clear what was right by giving these laws. We knew they could not keep these laws and any attempt would be filled with pain and failure for them. So we encouraged them to only focus on the action, not the attitude. What was the right action you needed to do to be right. We flamed the desire for control and the discomfort of pain and wrong attitudes and used these to try to get them to justify themselves using actions as the standard, not attitudes.

Let me give you an example. One of the laws was, 'Remember the Sabbath day to keep it holy.' This one simple law became 24 chapters of rules with one group. In another group it became 156 pages of rules.

How did we get these human vermin to do it? The law says that there must be no work on the Sabbath. We stirred the subjects to ask: 'What is work?' Work is then defined under 39 different headings which are called 'fathers of work.' One of the things which are forbidden is the carrying of a burden. Immediately the subject asks: 'What is a burden?' So in their writing there is definition after definition of what constitutes a burden — mild enough for a gulp, honey enough to put on a sore, oil enough to anoint the smallest member (which is further defined as the little toe of a child one day old) water enough to rub off an eye-plaster, leather enough to make an amulet, ink enough to write two letters of the alphabet, coarse sand enough to cover a plasterer's trowel, reed enough to make a pen, a pebble big enough to throw at a bird, anything which weighs as much as two dried figs. [1] On and on go the regulations, never ending.

Like a noose slowly being drawn around their necks, they hang themselves with the very tool our enemy gave them. Why do they do this? They have a compulsive desire to be right or at least, appear to be right. Since they have joined our side they have a sense of guilt as a result of their breaking from the enemy and they must find some way to deal with this. We help them by convincing them to think they won't be guilty if their actions are 'right' even when their hearts are wrong. It is a wonderful trap that we have used on millions upon millions of them. Thus they spend all their time trying to find exactly what is the right action in every situation.

I can already hear your whining, whimpering squeaky little voice say, 'But my subject is not a religious leader, how does this apply to him?' I am learning to anticipate your simple-mindedness and so I will explain this in terms you can understand.

The human scum in your subject's organiza-tion all have a desire to be right (or at least to appear right) and to do the right thing. For all creation, to be right is to be safe and protected. For the scum in your subject's organization they will think that if they do their jobs right, if they do the right work, then they will be safe and not be fired. When fear rules in an organi-zation, as it often does during change, then they will do the same thing in the organization that the religious leaders did. The fearful scum will seek to define and create more and more rules of action for every situation they find themselves in. They will think that if they always do what is right in their jobs, they cannot be fired, blamed, shamed or become vulnerable.

Soon the actions they have defined as right become what everyone must do and they are then trapped in the rules they have created and they begin to die and the organization dies with them.

Your aware friend,
Wyrmwud

From: <Wyrmwud> wyrmwud@hell.edu
To: <Tweazel> tweazel@hell.edu
Subject: <u>Modern leaders</u>

Tweazel,

You write of your subject's frustration in having too little time to do what he wants or feels like he should do. After opening three new offices around the country he is overwhelmed. Everybody brings their crises or problems to him and wants him to solve them all. Excellent.

You will of course be aware that in an organization that is run like a machine there is only one individual who can fix the machine. That is the mechanic; in this case, your subject. The leader is the only true mechanic and thus believes he is the only one who can decide what needs to be done. Obviously the parts can't fix the machine. Thus all problems must come to him and you have him on the run.

Your subject will be dragged in many different directions and I trust you have convinced him that he is the only one who knows what is going on and thus must deal with all the problems himself. As much as he says he dislikes it, you can feed his ego and encourage his pride as he enjoys the hidden pleasure of being needed and thus irreplaceable. He will be stressed or burned out and this will open the door for him to try and find some form of comfort. You of course will provide many opportunities for women, drugs, drinking or entertainment that will be available to him to ease the pain. Let me emphasize the word again, use 'entertainment' as it is a culturally acceptable way to escape.

I am learning that I cannot assume anything with your limited brain size so I will state the obvious. Since he is the only one who can make decisions or fix anything, it will make those in his organization more dependent on him and less confident in themselves. This will create a vicious circle. Because he has to make all the decisions he will assume his workers are incompetent. They will assume he doesn't trust them and will lose any sense of ownership in the decisions made. He will sense this and make more decisions and they will feel more and more untrusted and thus incompetent. On and on the circle goes. This can only ruin the relationships and will eventually destroy the organization.

I read from your notes that you seem to enjoy his stress and confusion. Do you not understand the element that brings all of this on is change? Or maybe I should clarify it and say the speed of change. For reasons we do not fully understand, the human vermin are affected by change. I mentioned this earlier in regards to death but it is not limited to that. Their world is bound by time and change seems to deeply affect them. They enter their world as small dependent creatures and throughout their lives watch as they grow older and stronger and then lose this strength and become weaker and weaker. They lose their hair, teeth and shape all in the name of time and change. We have a whole team of researchers working on it and exploring how we can use it to our advantage. We do know we can use their fear of change in regards to how they lead and organize themselves.

In earlier years when the length of the leader's life span was much shorter, he didn't have to worry much about change because he would die before he had to deal with it. Change was seen as a slow moving process that he could usually avoid if he wanted to. This is no longer true and the vermin now know or will soon know that every one of them must learn to deal with change. Our filthosophers have warned us that this has the appearance of the work of our enemy. They tell us that this will force the human vermin to not trust in their world and will open the door to dependence on the hated one. The enemy has written that anything that can be shaken will be shaken and we believe it is because of the speed of change that confronts them. One of the things we do know is that when they are confronted with change and thus uncertainty, their first response is to get defensive and to pull back and protect them-selves. They will often plant their heels and refuse to move forward. Use this for your advantage.

Let me remind you, you will not have access to new subjects unless you can get your current subject to fear change, uncertainty and risk and to cling to what he is comfortable with -- namely the past. This will stop any growth and cut him off from the enemy as we know the enemy has stated that he has specific plans to change the little vermin. You have your work before you, just do it or else.

Another reminder, keep your subject ignorant about the speed of change and the importance of adaptation as long as you can because the organization he is building will not be able to adapt to change. It was established with stability in mind but he won't know that. Let me say this clearly so you don't miss my point. Machines can't adapt. They are made for a stable environment and thus in a changing world, quickly become obsolete. This will severely limit your subject, as he will spend enormous energy trying to get a machine to adapt when it can't. I will write soon of a strategy that we are currently refining. I just want to check out our latest reports before I spell it out to you.

Your well-informed friend,
Wyrmwud

From: <Wyrmwud> wyrmwud@hell.edu
To: <Tweazel> tweazel@hell.edu
Subject: <u>Identity and change</u>

Tweazel,

Your subject's push to get clearly defined job
descriptions for everyone, his frustration with
others' incompetence, his anxiety and defen-
siveness all seem to show his struggle with an
unstable world. He still has no idea that it is all
linked to the dilemmas inherent in dealing
with change. Although you have not written it,
I sense he will try and find absolutes as he
believes these will be his only hope of security.
As our enemy has placed within him a sense
that identity is the only absolute, make sure
and have him look inside himself or to others
as a misdirection. Do not let him think for even
a moment that the only absolute is the identity
of our enemy. You will have heard of our
enemy's promises to them that he will not
change, don't let your subject try and find
security in who the enemy is. I have written
earlier about this, review those notes. Remember our mission statement. I am sure you have
forgotten it so here it is again, "Our mission is
to attack, destroy, defame, slander, smear,
blame, insult, slur, dishonor, belittle, criticize,
denounce, berate, castigate, lie about and find
fault with the nature and character of our
enemy."

It is official. Our Exalted Founder Below has given the approval for us to begin to reveal ourselves to the human vermin. We are able to come out of the closet, so to say. Before you do something stupid, let me tell you the strategy behind this so you don't get me in trouble again.

There is a small but growing frustration among some businessmen and those who study organizations. A few have even begun to realize the weakness of organizing around the model of a machine. Our researchers anticipated this and we have begun to adjust our strategy to match their realization. As they begin to rethink how to better organize themselves we plan to use it to open new doors for us.

Snigglewart, Toiletry and Blinder have key subjects who are recognized as authorities in their field of leadership and organizational development. They are on the cutting edge of our work and have helped their subjects to see the problem is with the speed of change and the mind-set of a machine. We are also working extra hard on the enemy's slaves to confuse them so they don't see what the problem is. We do not want our subjects to think the enemy has anything to say about organization. We will keep the enemy's slaves wrestling with the problem of fixing the machine for as long as we can, thus it will give our subjects time to come to our conclusions. It is projected that we should have 5 to 10 years before the enemy's slaves are aware of what is happening. Fortunately for you there are not many philosophers in the enemy's camp from the business world and we seem to have things under control.

As I said, a few of our key subjects have begun to question that the model of a machine may not be the only way to view organizations. They know an organization must be flexible enough to adapt to the constant change that is confronting them and yet strong enough in regards to knowing its identity so as to be clear about what it can and cannot do. We are also helping them to see that the world is not all independent pieces but is linked together as some sort of living thing. A few of the really smart ones realize that their 'objective' truth is biased and that the world is not a machine but possibly a living organism. As they think their world might be alive, we are pushing with all our might for them to see that living things have a spirit.

And that my ignorant friend is where we come in. We will reveal ourselves as the unnamed spirit that keeps the world alive and guides them. Some of the vermin have called the movement 'New Age.' On a side note, don't you love the foul creatures who call our participation with them 'New' as if we were a new thing they have just discovered? Anyway, we are not to reveal ourselves with a specific name, but more as if we are an impersonal force. Let them think the force is with them. For now we are pushing them towards our work in eastern religions as the impersonal spirit at work in the world. You will even notice we have the symbol of Yin/Yang in business advertisements. We are promoting it as the symbol of life, balance and harmony. Some of our leading subjects are running to these facades we have built to answer their questions about building a living organization with a spirit. One that can grow and adapt to the changing world. Soon they will declare that objective reality is an illusion. They will follow our leading to be connected with us as a force and allow us to freely work in their midst.

As you are probably not aware, our battle is very difficult here and we must be extremely careful. One wrong move could be disastrous. If the enemy's slaves realize he uses the model of a body as the highest form of organization they will have a voice that many other subjects may be willing to listen to. This could interest them in our enemy and the open door to the spirit will lead them to him.

Push hard for mysticism and eastern religion to be the answer as your subject talks with other leading businessmen and researchers. Don't let him think that our enemy has anything to say, other than his own assumption which we have established, that an organization is a machine.

Whisper to him that letters written thousands of years ago cannot possibly have anything to say to modern organizations.

On a side note, I have heard a rumor of some of our members trying to make the fraternity emblem a vulture. I doubt Our Exalted Founder Below will say anything about this as he is too busy to even consider such frivolity. However, if he does get involved it will not be pretty. I suggest you do not get involved in silliness as we have more serious work to do.

Your vulturous friend,
Wyrmwud

From: <Wyrmwud> wyrmwud@hell.edu
To: <Tweazel> tweazel@hell.edu
Subject: A body

My dear Tweazel,

Your stupidity is alarming. If you weren't in
my organization I would laugh at your foolishness. Your subject is beginning to talk about the
body as a form of organization and you are not
terrified? Watch this with utmost care for your
future success lies in your ability to keep him
in the dark. Haven't you read anything I have
emailed you? You should be able to keep this
thinking from him for 5 to 10 years.

Work to make your subject limit his talk about
a body, to only think of it in a religious, mysti-
cal sense of relating to the enemy. If you do
your work well, he will have no idea it is the
basis for how they are to organize. Do not let
him think it applies to business. Push him to
keep it a mysterious idea that only fits in once
a week meetings with the enemy.

I realize you, and for that matter all of us in the
fraternity, have no frame of reference for organizing with the vermin's body as the model
because the idea is totally foreign and completely disgusting to us. However, this is no
excuse for your incompetence in understanding what the enemy declares is his intention.

Our filthosophers have made some clear comparisons that you should be aware of. Grow up and get serious. As disgusting as it sounds I will try and explain how a body operates as an organizing system. I will have to use some of the enemy's language in my description as we have no words in our own vocabulary to define an organization as a body.

• A body is a living system. It is a container that holds life. It grows and alters itself based on the environment it is working in. It is creative and can adapt when confronted with change. It even has the ability to heal itself when it is hurt.

• A body needs feedback from its environment to know how it is doing. Clear communication is vital. It is through communication that it can learn and grow.

• Organs are irreplaceable and the loss of an organ is a loss for the whole. Their medical vermin have replaced some of the vermin's organs but even then the patients have to take medicine their whole life so their body won't reject it. Organs are not interchangeable. They each have a place that no other organ can take. You cannot make an eye into a toe nail just to keep the body moving. Every organ is desperately needed for safety and survival.

I trust you sense the revulsion I have in writing these words out. Our only hope is that the model of a body as a container allows us access into their world. The greater the possibility for our use of it, the greater the possibility for the enemy's use of it. It is a risk Our Founder Below is willing to take if we are to destroy their world. I must keep moving on as there is more.

• The body is more than the sum of its parts. You cannot understand it by breaking it down into pieces. It can only be understood as a whole system of relationships. The relationships of the parts to each other are extremely important. As they work together the body can do amazing things.

• A body has a head that functions as a servant for order. It does not control or dictate commands, but knows that any pain in the body is carried in the head. The head and the heart are inseparable.

• A body has value in what it is, and cannot be used and thrown away. It does not exist to only produce, but is made for a relationship. Each body is unique and has a beauty all its own.

As I write this I feel my wrath rising to dangerous levels. Do you understand now the importance of how they think about organization? I cannot even bear the thought that you cannot see how this ties in. I will try and write out some thoughts if my anger at your lack of understanding doesn't distract me too much.

• If the organization can adapt, then the leader is free to serve and not control. Everyone doesn't have to come to him as he is not the only one who knows what to do. Your subject would realize that each of the vermin are needed and can adapt and heal themselves with the help of other vermin.

• If communication is taking place, then they have the capacity to share from their hearts and understand each other. With communication taking place they can also listen to the human parasites in the city or country they are in and adapt to meet their needs.

• If they realize that every vermin is different and unique and must be in the right place working with the right vermin, then the vermin are valued and cannot be discarded when they are sick or weak.

• If the relationships are a priority among the vermin, then the body is functioning and its power is way beyond the power of the group of individual subjects.

• If a leader doesn't have to control or dominate, then he doesn't have to be the mechanic. He will realize that pain in another vermin is his pain. He will also realize that subjects have an authority and responsibility in their own areas that they need to operate in.

- If each organization is different, then each has a value and beauty all its own.

If the fraternity is the head, then we can control the body. If the enemy is the head then he controls it. If you can't see how this changes everything, then you are out of my organization and you can count on a personal visit from me which you will never forget. Do your homework or face my wrath.

Your disgusted friend,
Wyrmwud

From: <Wyrmwud> wyrmwud@hell.edu
To: <Tweazel> tweazel@hell.edu
Subject: <u>Conflict</u>

Tweazel,

You wrote on and on in your last email about
all the fights, disagreements and battles you
are starting. I wish you would just come out
and say that there is conflict there and you are
working closely with it. You seem to be as
narrow-minded as your subject if you think
that any conflict is an automatic victory for our
side. I wish you had listened more in school so
I wouldn't have to do the work of your pre-
school teacher.

I will not take much time now because I have
an enjoyable job ahead of me as one of my
long-term subjects is close to dying. Of course,
I want to be with him to welcome him to my
side. I so enjoy the first look they have when
they see me and I welcome them. You can see
all the lies and illusions used to protect themselves wither and die before them at the horror
of my appearance. As I reach over and chain
them to me for all eternity, their first primor-
dial scream at what is happening is like a
symphony to my ears. A rare and expensive
gift received from a friend in their world could
not bring as much pleasure to them as this
moment does to me. There is nothing that
compares with that first scream. Maybe some

day you will taste of this delight. Unfortunately, soon it settles into a dull aching noise from them and I find my hunger for more 'living food' returning. I believe the more I hear and partake of their measly little souls, the hungrier I become. It is not a pleasant thought to think the more I partake, the more I become addicted. In the end, it is well worth that one moment when their scream is at its freshest.

Now, quickly back to my one point before I must run. One of your main tasks is to reinforce over and over the belief that any conflict means something is wrong. Once this is established, link it so that tension is seen as the same thing as conflict. You want your subject to assume that when there is tension, it means that something is wrong and it must be dealt with.

A particularly useful tool is to make him feel responsible for any form of tension. The unspoken ingredient is that it is his fault. You can help him see that if he were just a better leader, there would be no tension.

Work on his being responsible for all tension and conflicts and I will write more when I get back.

Your soon-to-be full friend,
Wyrmwud

From: <Wyrmwud> wyrmwud@hell.edu
To: <Tweazel> tweazel@hell.edu
Subject: <u>Tension</u>

Tweazel,

If I hadn't enjoyed the last scream so much you can be assured I would be mad. But even your ignorance cannot take that pleasure from me. For a short while, I don't even mind writing to you. The fresh meal has given me new strength to deal with you.

You wrote of the tension between your subject and other leaders in his organization. You have not pushed it directly into conflict. You seem content with only tension and obviously did not hear me in my last email to you. I will put this in caps so you will know I am screaming at you, IF THERE IS TENSION IN AN ORGANIZATION IT USUALLY MEANS THAT THERE IS LIFE AND THEY ARE GROWING. This is not what we want. It is so obvious that you have not studied organizations as this is the most basic element of organizational life. Our filthosophers tell us that tension is a sign that the human scum are working together and there is an allowance for differences among themselves. Tension is the mechanism that keeps them in contact with each other and causes growth. It is a by-product of the enemy's presence that you must distort. Tweazel, get a grip. Our enemy made them so that there would be tension and thus growth in a group. Think about it, how else could there be a variety of different gifts and motivations unless they were all coordinated through tension?

On a positive note your subject does not understand the importance of tension or seem to know how to deal with it. You have done well in convincing him that if there is tension, something is wrong and as the leader, it is his fault. I see you have also kept your subject from talking with other leaders about the small tensions that bother him. This is where the battle is fought. Issues become big and deliciously destructive through small issues that have not been dealt with. Our Exalted Founder Below's guidelines clearly state that our focus with the human vermin is to try and convince them that small issues don't matter. A minor misunderstanding, a harsh word, difference of opinion, procrastination or whatever the small 'idiosyncrasies' are, they don't need to be talked about or bothered with. Work at convincing him they are irrelevant and will only slow things down as things seem to be working now. A common phrase we have used among them is, "Don't rock the boat."

Once this mentality is created in your subject then your work will be much easier. These small issues ooze emotions into their relationships and if given time, they will almost certainly ferment. I can see this has happened and you have begun to taste the joy of a subject's collected and stored emotions that have soured and gone bad.

I am sure the taste was sweet and a pleasure you are not used to. I have heard certain vermin say they can feel the presence of these emotions but I am not sure that is true. It may be they are just feeling our presence as we hover over and stir the anger, injustice, envy, jealousy and strife. Your subject cannot hold these emotions inside forever so you must look for the most opportune time in order to have him dump the emotions on others. When your subject is stuffed and stirred with these feelings, you can provoke him with the slightest push and he will let loose with all the energy of a vomiting volcano. It is during these times that he will say the most destructive things as he will be overcome with the feelings he has stored up. Our researchers have discovered that the vermin usually store up the emotions and then draw strength from them to finally deal with difficult situations. They only deal with things when they feel strongly about them. This can work to our advantage.

When you get your subject to vent all these stirred up emotions others will be overwhelmed. Let there be an awkwardness with it so they don't talk about it. Let it become undiscussable among the vermin. This will produce fear, wonderfully life-killing fear, in their midst as those around him will not know when it will happen again and thus will be insecure. (Do you remember this word from earlier? Use it to your advantage.)

If the disgusting creatures do talk about it, direct their conversation to see that venting emotions is being 'open and honest' with each other. You must be very careful to reinforce our definition of openness and honesty. I am pleased to say these words have been carefully crafted over the years by our word masters to mean little of their original meaning.

As I am sure you will not know our work in this area let me briefly describe it. Openness and honesty have been crafted to mean sharing feelings with other vermin that are hurtful to them. Our focus has been to help them vent their feelings in such a way that it is full of generalities, distortions and deletions. When this happens it is assured that nobody can learn anything from it and the relationships are weaker because of it.

Your attentive friend,
Wyrmwud

From: <Wyrmwud> wyrmwud@hell.edu
To: <Tweazel> tweazel@hell.edu
Subject: <u>Dilemmas</u>

Tweazel

I did mention the word dilemma earlier and I
was wondering if your minuscule mind had
any idea of what I was talking about. As I
suspected, you are ignorant again in an area
that is vital for your ability to guide your
subject.

I am sure in your puny thinking process that
problems and dilemmas are the same thing.
You are wrong again. Dilemmas are not just
complex problems. The way you are thinking
is how you want your subject to think, not how
you should be thinking! My stupid fiend, there
is a huge difference between a problem and a
dilemma and you must understand it in order
to try and destroy your subject. I do wonder if
there is any hope for you to ever sink lower
than you are now.

In its simplest form problems are situations
where you know or can discover what you
need to know. There is a logical, clear, know-
able answer. Once you find the answer, you
can solve the problem.

Dilemmas are paradoxes that cannot be solved
once and for all. In vermin terms, they are the

result of two or more good things you want to accomplish and when one is chosen there is a loss of another. They are connected to each other and they must be reconciled or decided over and over again. They are never dealt with by a single choice. Let me make this real practical. You are a dilemma to me. I have much destruction I want to bring through you, but you are young and stupid and I don't know what to do with you. Do I hope that you will produce one day for me and thus give my precious energy to you or do I give up that hope and consume you and enjoy that pleasure? It is a choice I must make every time I hear from you.

Dilemmas are what create the tension in an organization or group. They are the life of the group. In order to understand how these dilemmas work, think of what the vermin call walking. They have two legs and it is both legs working together that moves the body forward. First the movement of one leg, then the movement of the other. I think a better phrase for walking should be ordered imbalance. Another example that comes to my mind is the flight of a bird. It takes both wings working in tension with each other to create flight.

Your goal with your subject is to have him make all dilemmas into problems. He will then assume he can make a decision once and for all and the problem should go away. This will cause him to swing to one side and polarize on issues and the result will be that many of the human scum will be hurt and there is the potential for a split in your subject's organization.

Let me give you some examples. Two key values for any organization are relationships and performance. If you relate well with others you can perform better. Challenge your subject to emphasize performance and to not consider the vermin and their relationships. Another two values are risk and stability. The more stable and safe the organization is to work in the more the people will be willing to take risks. Push your subject to take wild risks and to forget completely about stability. This will make everybody insecure. Another area I wrote you about earlier is in identity. For an organization it is made up of both group and individual identity. If he emphasizes only the group he will get conformity and the creativity of a group comes through the individual. If he focuses only on the individual then you would only have a collection of individuals and no organization. I have heard it said that, that is like herding a group of cats. Another area has to do with vision and reality. Get him to focus completely on the vision and deny any sense of reality.

He will constantly feel the challenge of these and many more dilemmas as he tries to lead.

Get him to think that freedom from the tension would come if he could swing to one side of the dilemma and make a decision once and for all and thus remove the tension it causes in him. You can guess what would happen if you can get him to do this. Think of a one-legged man or a one-winged bird and you have your answer.

Push the idea of balance. Get your subject to think that any slave of our enemy should only be interested in balance. Let him think this means the complete removal of tension. In the example of a vermin walking, you can't be balanced and walk at the same time. It is the actual imbalance that brings movement. So it is in groups. Don't let your subject see this. Have him strive for balance in all things and it will slowly bring the movement and life in his organization to a halt.

I think this is enough for now as I want to hear from you to see if you have any idea what I am writing about.

Your friend who is under a lot of tension,
Wyrmwud

From: <Wyrmwud> wyrmwud@hell.edu
To: <Tweazel> tweazel@hell.edu
Subject: <u>Division</u>

Tweazel

I see you have made an attempt to understand what I am saying but it was feeble at best. Let me spell it out clearly in another way for you.

We accept there is tension in any group. Our filthosophers have stated there is nothing we can do with this but work with it.

For your subject in any given day there will be tension. Misdirect it. We believe the enemy put tension there to allow them to raise questions and understand themselves and their world better. The answers and understanding come about because of their natural desire to solve tension. Our Exalted Founder Below has revealed this cruelty of the enemy in giving the vermin a desire to remove tension and yet also creating them so that their survival depends upon there being tension.

With tension there will always be questions. The enemy revealed this to us when he first entered the garden when Adam and Eve joined our side. His first response was to ask, "Where are you?" It was then we knew how important questions were in dealing with tension. When questions are raised because of the tension, your work is to influence the questions to appear to be a challenge rather than a desire to learn. These questions will bring out insecurity in the leader. If this happens you can turn the tension into conflict. What was an opportunity for our enemy to teach them to learn and communicate with each other has become our chance to separate them.

Our researchers have discovered that one of the key ways the enemy tries to work is through the vermin's mind. I think in the enemy's words, he wants them to transform themselves by the renewing of their minds. So we know our attack has to misdirect this focus. We believe the enemy wants them to bring their beliefs into the open through the questions asked.

What he would label as false beliefs can then be corrected when they are exposed. We know the human scum hate self-awareness, especially when it exposes them. They will easily listen to you to focus on actions. Make them think beliefs are irrelevant. We have found a very favorable attack is to push for polarization. Feed those in the organization the assumption that if one group is right, then it is automatically assumed that the other group is wrong. It is either one or the other, it cannot be both. You do remember that a dilemma has at least two sides, sometimes more. Thus you help them break all dilemmas apart.

This is where you can push for balance and thus by the use of this word, create extremes on either side. One group needs to state their views stronger than even they believe in order to balance out the other group. The other group will of course state their views stronger still to balance out the strong views that were shared. They will each pull harder and harder like a tug-of-war. As a result of this, you can work at building two camps that see each other as the problem. Don't let them see they are both concerned with the same area but with a different emphasis.

Even your pathetic little brain can see that this opens the door for division among them. Where the enemy wants unity and synergy, we bring forth division and loneliness. Oh the beauty of taking the desires our enemy has placed within them and using it for our good. The wisdom of Our Exalted Founder Below brings forth our victory. As the enemy is trying to bring unity around the identity of the hated one, you can bring division through polarization. The tension the enemy uses for life, we misdirect to bring death.

Your masterful friend,
Wyrmwud

From: \<Wyrmwud\> wyrmwud@hell.edu
To: \<Tweazel\> tweazel@hell.edu
Subject: <u>Character</u>

Tweazel,

I was able to intercept a note you were trying to pass on to internal affairs about my lack of willingness to help you. You seem to think I should have told you much earlier about polarization and that it would have been much easier to apply to your subject when he was younger. I would agree, but you are so intellectually challenged and would not even have understood it if I tried. I do try and work within your limitations. Do not try and undermine me again or I shall put you back where I found you where your only contact with the vermin is the freedom given you on our night of celebration on Oct. 31. Your punishment for your foolishness is that you must write out our mission statement a thousand times and then crawl to me with the papers in your mouth. You are to come to me and drop it in my hand and then kiss my deliciously dirty feet. I will be waiting.

Now, back to business. The last note you wrote actually had an intelligent thought in it. Too bad you were sucking up to me in it. I know you were trying to distract me while you went to internal affairs. You tried to link tension to character. If I had not intercepted the note I

135

would have been encouraged with your progress. I told you I would be watching you.

Why do you not see the importance our enemy places on character? You seem to think it is your idea that we should focus on attacking and weakening the character. Our enemy has declared that the vermin's character is the defining line for those who want leadership. If you hadn't noticed, tension is the reason why the enemy puts so much emphasis on character. He knew they would need character to be able to carry the tension that confronts all leaders.

Character is what gives the vermin the ability to carry tension and not divide a group. With the dilemmas and thus tension involved in leadership you can see why we put so much effort into weakening or destroying the vermin's character. As you seem to be unclear what character is, let me use an illustration that might give you understanding.

Character is like a box. It is the package in which the tensions of life are held. The stronger the character in the vermin, the more tension they can carry, the more influence, wisdom and power the enemy seems to give them. Let me say it again, character is like a box, the stronger it is the more it can carry. Your subject's character is the box that carries the tension of the different relationships and giftings that are needed in an organization. You must work to weaken or destroy the box.

I noticed you have used one of our favorite reasoning processes on your subject. Since he is convinced there is absolute truth, and he proclaims to know the truth, you are at work to convince him that everything he knows is absolutely true.

This is a great way to get the human scum to polarize because they think that if they yield in their view they are yielding truth and compromising. Do not let him think that what he knows is filtered through his culture, family, experiences and personality and that he only sees a part of the truth. Why even the cursed one Paul wrote that he saw things dimly as through a glass.

I have noticed you seem to be trying to use this to open the door and bring confusion in your subject by undermining his idea of absolutes. If he knows the truth and truth is supposed to be absolute, yet what he knows isn't absolutely true, then push him to think that truth is not absolute. Do not let him think that truth is held in a container like water in a glass. As long as it is in the container it is in the right place. Two different particles of water can be right and in different places.

As a slave of the enemy your subject will be aware of the enemy's claims of knowing absolutes and you have done well to ridicule them. Of course you know we are at a disadvantage here as no finite creation can know what is unchanging or absolutely true. Any statements we accept as true must be accepted on faith based on who we think knows the most. We know the enemy cannot be trusted as he has all power and is thus selfish to only want his will. Thus Our Founder Below is the best guide.

I fear I have written too much. Humor me and write and tell me the part communication plays in all this.

Waiting for some sign of intelligence. . .

Your hopeful friend,
Wyrmwud

From: <Wyrmwud> wyrmwud@hell.edu
To: <Tweazel> tweazel@hell.edu
Subject: <u>Communication</u>

Tweazel,

You did well to remember that the enemy breathed them into existence and thus they have power in their words. I was hoping you would be able to tie together the part communication plays in misdirecting tension, but you didn't.

The only way your subject can use tension to grow is to communicate and talk openly about the tension and expose his own heart in the process. If you want to understand the importance of communication and their words, read the enemy's letters to them. Our researchers continue to press on us that distorting their communication is one of our primary goals. In the midst of change, the only way the enemy can keep them growing is through clear communication. Work hard at distorting it. The key for you to remember is that the words they use, define the relationships they have and thus how they organize themselves. Only those organizations that learn to communicate will be able to adapt to change.

On a side note, work on your subject's ideals and how others see them expressed. Let me give you an example from a marriage I was working on with one of my subjects. The ideal he declared was love. He expressed this disgusting attribute to his wife by bringing her flowers. I was able to link love to a specific action of flowers given and when he stopped bringing her flowers she accepted my ideas that he stopped loving her. This then hindered communication and thus, I was able to break up the marriage in the end all because of this simple rule used over and over. It works just as well among those in an organization. Use it.

Your subject will communicate his ideals to his employees and will try to link them to concrete actions or behaviors so that those under him will see what he means. They will blindly link his ideals to specific actions. You don't have to even worry about twisting the ideals, just tie them to specific actions. These actions then take on the meaning of the ideals. Soon you can remove the vulgar ideals and focus only on actions. Those in the organization will then consider it right to act in a certain way if you want to be a part of the organization. Anyone who acts differently will be cut off. This will lead to arthritic rigidity, swinging polarization and high wall impasses which, as you know, will kill any organization.

Your destructive friend,
Wyrmwud

From: <Wyrmwud> wyrmwud@hell.edu
To: <Tweazel> tweazel@hell.edu
Subject: <u>FWD</u>

Tweazel,

I have forwarded a witch's recipe that you
could find helpful. You might try and use it as
it presents some of the areas we have been
dealing with in our communication. She is not
a teacher at the Deceiver's School so it is rough,
but she has captured a part of our work. I
suggest you post it next to your computer so
you can read it every day. You should be able
to cause a split without even having to think
about it. It should become second nature to
you.

———————— Forwarded Message ————————

From: <Bentnose> bentnose@hell.edu
To: <Wyrmwud> wyrmwud@hell.edu
Subject: <u>Recipe for destruction</u>

A Recipe for Destruction

The most important ingredient, thankfully, is
the easiest to find. Gather a bunch of small
frustrations, little misunderstandings, a series
of harshly spoken words, or just the appearance of evil. It is very important that they not

be talked about and are not exposed to the light of the relationship, as this will rob them of their evil power.

As they are gathered and stored, allow the emotions and tensions that are associated with them to sit quietly and stew. On their own they may mean little, but mix them up and they provide a catalyst for feelings of anger, bitterness and envy to settle in and grow. Give these feelings time to spoil and try and forget exactly where they came from. Allow them to be hidden under the mask of insignificance, or not wanting to upset things when they are going well, or just that they will be dealt with later at a better time.

After they have stewed for a time and there are strong emotions, wait until there is a new situation with the person and then dump all the emotions on them. Be sure and allow all the energy from the emotions to be vented and don't say specifically where the feelings came from. Influence the person to share generalities with distortions and deletions woven into the words.

Have them apologize for the outburst and then pretend like it didn't happen. Cover it up quickly and just get on with life, hoping that things will return to "normal." As time passes, make this situation undiscussable.

Let this same process happen several times in the same way stated above and continue to cover it up and try to get back to "normal" as quickly as possible. Use these blow-ups to create an atmosphere of fear as those involved never know when the person is going to lose it again.

This last process is very delicate and must be handled carefully. You want the difficulty to change from issues, weaknesses or dilemmas to become a personality or a leadership-style problem. The key point is that the person is now seen as the problem. Work with this so thoughts that sound like, "They are always saying negative things," quickly move to, "They are such a negative person." Once this bridge is crossed then it becomes easier and easier to see the person as the problem. When this happens anything the person does can be written off because "he" is the problem.

The next and final step is the accomplishment of all your hard work. The only way to resolve a personal problem with someone is to leave or make them leave. At the very least it is to withhold love from them and to keep your distance. People don't want to and can't live together with others when they know their very existence with you or the group will cause problems. People or groups splitting up is the next obvious step from here and with it you have finished your recipe.

Remember my dear, the process is the same for a small group as it is for a nation. It is particularly fun in a nation as you turn group against group and allow the hatred to simmer and spoil for generation after generation. Soon the people will remember nothing but their hatred for the other group. In this way millions can be destroyed in one beautiful sweep of war.

——— End of forwarded message ———

I trust you have enjoyed the recipe.

Your friend who is a master chef,
Wyrmwud

From: <Wyrmwud> wyrmwud@hell.edu
To: <Tweazel> tweazel@hell.edu
Subject: Integrity

Tweazel,

Your struggle to get him to swear, go to porno
movies or tell a dirty joke reveals that you
seem to think that if you can just tempt your
subject to make a wrong choice, then he will
not have integrity. You seem to model the very
simple-mindedness I am trying to get you to
work in your subject. Tweazel, get serious. Try
and put more than one thought together at a
time. What you are struggling with is what you
want your subject to struggle with. Have him
be the fool and not yourself. A wrong choice is
a small piece of breaking his integrity, giving
him a wrong mindset is a master piece in
breaking his integrity.

Our wordsmiths tell us that the vermin's
meaning of the word integrity comes from the
noun 'integer,' which signifies wholeness,
entirety, completion. So if the vermin are going
to think and act with integrity they must see
the big picture and integrate the multiple
perspectives of a complex world. I realize I
have just lost your mustard seed-sized brain so
let me tie this in with what I have written
before.

In order to destroy your subject's integrity you must work at limiting how he views the world. You must also restrict his capacity to hold and experience the tensions placed on him through other vermin's so-called gifts and abilities. The enemy states that true integrity is found in the mind. And in case you're stupider than I think, the mind will only define and accept that which the heart is willing to embrace. You do not want him to link his heart and his mind together. That would be a horrifying form of integrity that would bring on you the wrath of the internal investigators.

Our filthosophers have tried to convince us that the enemy desires for his slaves to be whole. I am assuming this linking of heart and mind is a key part of what they mean. If you have listened to our wordsmiths you will know that 'health', 'wholeness' and 'holiness' all have the same root meaning.

Now, let me spell out our attack. Our researchers have discovered through millions of trials that the vermin who will fulfill our desires and accomplish evil are those that see things in only one narrow way. They are a delicious group who do not like to think, and are unwilling to deal with difficult issues, expose certain feelings or tolerate pain or guilt. They quickly set out to destroy those who would embrace any other view but their own. Religious vermin seem to be the most open to this. The Pharisees were an excellent model and we were able to use them to kill the hated one.

I will try and say this clearly. If you want to destroy your subject's integrity then you must get him to see only one side of the picture. Convince him that dilemmas are intolerable. Let him think one-sided cures — spend more on marketing, work harder, be creative, cut expenses, keep tight control — will automatically bring success.

You must narrow his thinking through his unwillingness to carry a group's tensions. Keep him from seeing complex dilemmas through contrasting perspectives. Work at convincing him that he should not have to carry unpleasant or conflicting feelings. See to it that his thinking is compartmentalized and fragmented. Persuade him that everyone around him must agree with him.

Thankfully, as I wrote earlier, the foundation for this has already been laid and is now a part of the vermin's educational system. Most of the human scum will naturally think this way because of the way they were educated. Without a bigger picture the smaller pieces of their lives will all be meaningless. They will not see how the pieces fit together. Think of a puzzle. Each of the pieces has meaning and a place only in context to the picture they are trying to create.

When your subject thinks as you are thinking, then and only then will you have truly destroyed his integrity.

Your big-picture friend,
Wyrmwud

From: <Wyrmwud> wyrmwud@hell.edu
To: <Tweazel> tweazel@hell.edu
Subject: <u>Inspection</u>

Tweazel,

I have just received an email from internal affairs that you are under investigation again. Your subject's continued success speaks badly of your training. I fear they will soon question me in greater depth because of your incompetence. Know this, I will not go down with you.

I am afraid you took literally what I said in the last email. I was not saying that you are to convince him that all religions are the same and that is what I meant by him seeing the big picture. You deserved to be laughed at by him when you tried to present the idea to his mind. He knows too much and will not fall for such a simplistic idea.

What I had hoped you would understand was that you needed to use the dilemmas in his life, organization and the enemy's writings to convince him that there was only one right way for anyone to be involved in the enemy's camp. That there is only one right way to organize. One right way to do business. One right way to . . . You finish the statement with whatever you sense his weakness is. Go back and read the notes I sent you on dilemmas. Maybe, just maybe they will make more sense now.

Your subject's organization is very large now and spread out. He is in three different countries with over 400 workers. You are going to have to lower yourself to a new level of attack if you are going to bring your leader's influence to a minimum. I will work with you a little more. If you cannot stop his influence, then I will be pleased to finish you off, once and for all.

As I write this, I have just received a high priority encrypted email from Our Exalted Founder Below. He is on the war path and has renewed plans for the days we are in. He senses time is running short and is consumed with making sure as many business, governmental, educational, or religious leaders as possible are under our influence. My schedule is going to be very busy for a while. I will not have time to babysit you and thus I need to see whether you can use the tools I have given to you to corrupt the subject's organization. Please summarize my work and tie the loose ends together.

You can consider this a test. Pass it and you will be given more opportunities. Fail it and you are my next meal.

Your very hungry friend,
Wyrmwud

From: <Wyrmwud> wyrmwud@hell.edu
To: <Tweazel> tweazel@hell.edu
Subject: <u>Your test</u>

Tweazel,

How can you say so little using so many
words? Your attempt to write out everything I
have written to you as answers for the test, in
the hope that you will hit on at least some of
the key ideas, is ridiculous. However, in light
of the amount of work there is to do, I will
accept your long email as an attempt at intelligence. Let me try and help one last time and
lay out the key ingredients that must be in the
mix of destruction.

Our goal is to create organizations that will
slowly and thoroughly suffocate the human
vermin. Until we are ready to instigate war, we
have found the greatest damage can come
through simple-minded vermin who will
blindly carry out their jobs with no concern for
how it affects anyone else.

What we want is a place where the human
vermin come and do a seemingly small and
apparently futile job that has no meaning to
them. Preferably a mindless job that requires
the same tasks done, day in and day out. Pa-
perwork shuffled between offices; baskets
filled and emptied with wasted time; computers logged onto and then wading through

lifeless emails; hours, weeks or even years spent at a job that nobody comments on, nobody notices and obviously nobody cares about. The only thing we have not done is to put bars on the windows and it would be the perfect jail. We have captured them and hold them captive all in the name of earning a living. Let them suffocate and then honor it by calling it a bureaucracy. Drink deeply of their agony my ignorant friend. I know it is slow in fermenting, but rich and flavorable in taste.

Hundreds of millions of souls, even as I write, waste their lives and lose their inheritance in the futility of what they try and honor by calling it work. They have long forgotten about their supposed gifting, and their pathetic passions have been anesthetized into a sleepy hopelessness. All in the name of responsibility, hard work and because our subjects as leaders organized them this way.

In order to achieve a rich mixture of agony, futility and hopelessness you must turn your subject to our side. The reason is because the leader is the one who determines the spirit of the organization. Because your subject has turned from us and joined the enemy's side, he has the potential to instill in it a life, culture and identity that will create a stench all the way to Our Exalted Founder Below. Caring and validating people, helping in the community, sharing wealth with employees are just a few of the things you must watch out for. Your subject will never be fully able to see people as we desire him to and there is always the risk that he will realize he's doing our dirty work in his organization. I know you will not let this happen, or else. If he cannot be turned to our side, be sure to plant efficient vermin below him who will limit your subject's influence and do our work for us all in the name of getting the job done. Very few of the enemy's slaves understand how we have influenced organizations to work.

The ability to use an organization is the true artistry of our fraternity and something through which much composure is needed. I am sure it is something you will never experience personally, but if you stay with me I will let you see the artistry of my work. I must confess when you see the long drawn out agony I can bring, it is breathtaking. Don't misunderstand me. All of us in the fraternity desire the blatant evil of groups that are not afraid of killing, destroying and raw violence. Oh that the whole world were a death camp.

Although this brings unspeakable pleasure to us, we have found its long-term consequences to be more damaging than good. It really is more an outbreak of those in our ranks who cannot control themselves than our agreed-upon strategy. Restraint is hard for us but has far greater rotten fruit among the vermin we have set out to destroy and thus we can get even with our enemy. Remember our mission statement.

So how would you use an organization for our purposes? Let me give you an example of how it might be done with your subject's organization.

Make the vermin in his organization constantly aware of the changes going on all around them. Have them read in the newspaper of widespread downsizing or mergers and how many people are losing their jobs. Have them watch it splashed all over the evening news. Emphasize how vulnerable they are and how quickly things can change if profits are down even a little bit. This will make them insecure as they become aware that their own jobs and positions may be pulled out from underneath them. Work with these feelings to create an environment of fear and instability. Thus, they will become compliant and do whatever is needed to keep their jobs.

Make sure the vermin identify each other and themselves by their role or title. Link the value of their identity to their positions. When you have done this, then if they lose their positions in the organization, they will feel like they are losing their identity and thus their value. Make sure everyone's job is carefully defined by a job description. These early seeds of specialization will produce strong weeds later as they deal with change.

Be sure your subject is unclear about where he wants the organization to go or what he wants it to be. Let him think that he operates by a gut instinct so he can't explain it to others. Convince him that the only thing that matters is that everybody fulfills their job descriptions.

As a reminder, this mentality is from the example of a machine. Get him to feel like he must make all the decisions and get everyone to bring their decisions to him. He must believe he is the only mechanic that can fix the machine.

The more he treats the vermin in his organization like parts in a machine, the less ownership and responsibility the vermin will have in the organization. The longer this happens, the more they will just turn up to do their eight hours of work in their pre-assigned jobs. This will produce a delicious apathy in them as they will see little or no meaning or value in their work. Place a banner in their minds and remind them to read it everyday.

IT DOESN'T MATTER.

Your subject will misinterpret their apathy and will respond to it by establishing more and more control which means he will have to create and then rely on more rules, procedures and policies. These become the only way things get done in the organization. I have one organization that has books of rules the length of a shelf. Occasionally we provoke the vermin to read it, but only to protect themselves and know how little they have to do.

After some time passes the machine will be firmly established. Continue to reinforce in the vermin that they are only responsible for their small place in the organization, nothing else. Break down the idea that each subject is responsible for the whole. Reduce each subject involved to the lowest common denominator. Break down any individuality or creativity. Once this is done then train into them obedience to their role. Convince them that they don't see the bigger picture and thus can't possibly know what is best. This produces genuinely blind obedience. They will do anything they are told without questioning it. Once this is established, those in the organization will have no conscience and thus the organization will have no conscience.

Remember, the more specialization the better. A good example of this is an organization that is a war machine. This is how the disgusting vermin would describe it: "Those who manufacture the bombs don't question how they are used. That is not their responsibility. The pilots that fly and drop the bombs don't decide

156

where. The generals that decide where to drop
the bombs didn't decide to start the war. The
president that decided to start the war is only
carrying out the will of the people. Each person
is only doing what they are supposed to do."
All of the disgustingly delicious vermin are
only doing their jobs and can pretend they are
not responsible for what happens.

After a number of years, those in the organization will have a sense of hopelessness. Over-
whelm them with thoughts like, 'Nothing is
going to change around here.' 'The way things
have been done is the way things will always
be done.' 'If I try to change the system I'll be
crushed by the system.'

Continue on with the work of our wordsmiths
in regards to convincing the human scum that
tension is the same as conflict. Work hard to
convince them that all tension should be cut off
immediately and is a sign of sickness or trouble
in the organization. DO NOT LET THEM SEE THAT
TENSION IS A SIGN OF LIFE IN A GROUP, THAT IT SIGNALS
THE NEED TO COMMUNICATE WITH EACH OTHER. If
they don't communicate, the tension will grow
into stress and then conflict. Convince the
simple-minded vermin that they are fragile
and conflict is too scary to deal with personally.
Let them think it is safer for the organization to
deal with it. Exhort them that only those in
power can deal with conflict. Reinforce that
conflict is a terrorizing experience and should

only be dealt with by the system or by those who have power. This will tempt them to trust in the system for help rather than people. It will also reinforce their helplessness and remind them that they must obtain power and control in the system.

As the system starts to strangle them, whisper to them the sweetness of denial. They won't know it but you can help lead them to their deaths in this way. Don't let them see it as denial. Work with our wordsmiths and call it hope. Convince them to hope in hope and trust in the goodness of the human vermin. Fool them into thinking that things aren't as bad as they appear.

One of our most exhilarating lies is that the organization can learn, adapt and change on its own. If we can get the senseless vermin to believe this, then they will think the organization can change without people changing. This is a wonderful tonic that relieves them of any responsibility to change themselves.

Because vermin learn from experience, let them assume that organizations will learn from experience as well. Don't let them see that in an organization the cause of a problem is often far removed from the effect. One person in one department makes a decision and somebody else in another department feels the effects. Few people see the linkage and fewer still learn anything. If someone does learn from the situation, it is rarely passed into the system. The system stays the same, as all machines do.

I know you want me to give you a paint-by-numbers set in how to destroy an organization. I cannot do that as it is true artistry. There are many different ways it can be done in different cultures and with different vermin and that is why it is recognized as such a high art. As I mentioned, the best I can offer is that I will allow you to watch my work and even throw you a few souls as tidbits if you do as I say. The agony and pain that can be brought against our enemy makes the patience needed well worth the effort.

Your overworked friend,
Wyrmwud

From: <Wyrmwud> wyrmwud@hell.edu
To: <Tweazel> tweazel@hell.edu
Subject: <u>Beware</u>

Tweazel,

I must warn you that Our Exalted Founder
Below made it very clear that the enemy is up
to something. All the fraternity is on full alert.
We believe we are on the edge of accomplish-
ing our goal for mankind and that is why the
enemy can't stand it. In these next few years
we believe we shall be able to populate our
homeland for eternity.

A brief reminder here for I know your memory
is short. We were in the same place in building
the Tower of Babel and our enemy stepped in
and confused their language so that we could
not accomplish what we wanted. The human
scum were split up all over the world. We are
now close to the same place. We have seen the
Internet created and this will allow them to
join together all over the world and most will
speak the same language. We must be on guard
for the enemy may want to use this for his own
purposes. This cannot be allowed to happen.
Whoever wins this next battle will receive the
spoils of generations and billions of souls.
Remember our mission statement.

Guard well the relationships of your leader
because if any of his friends turn it could mean

major losses to our work. You will then be mine if that happens.

It is time to prove my investment in you was worth it. Do it.

Your anticipating friend,
Wyrmwud

Appendix

From: <Wyrmwud> wyrmwud@hell.edu
To: <Lecturers> deceiverschool@hell.edu
Subject: <u>Student feedback</u>

Dear Lecturers at Deceiver's School,

I have been working with Tweazel, your former student and I realize there were some major points lacking in his education. As you well know, these points have been key strong-holds we have used for decades and yet my student had limited understanding of the place they have in our work. I am sure he was a rare student that did not learn these things and I do know that he is extremely inept. You are among the best trainers we have and I do appreciate your sending him to work with me. I have briefly outlined my ideas for you to be aware of as students are leaving your training.

Leadership 101: A leader is his position

A most basic stronghold that allows us to hold most organizations captive is the single lie that leaders are defined by the position they hold. Leaders will cling to a role as if their very lives depend on it, and this opens the door for politics, power plays and back stabbing that we must maintain in our work. Please reaffirm in your students that the usefulness of a leader's identity is only as helpful to us as its attachment to his position. Also, it allows us to portray change as a threat to who he is as human scum. If the vermin sense this threat then they will not be open to change.

Blame shifting 105: The system is the problem

Although it is a natural tendency of our subjects to blame others, we must never assume that this will always be the case. Your students must understand that the problem for our subjects is always out there. Someone else, or better yet, the system is the problem. They must understand the basics of building a system that will continue doing things 'the way they have always been done' and know the fundamentals of organizational death. I do know that this is a by-product of my first point but it must be said. May I also add a note of encouragement of our work in history and the power of breaking things down into parts so that no individual in the organization ever has a responsibility outside of his or her 'role' or 'position.'

Group Dynamics 201:
Giving them the illusion of being in control

I do know that you have worked hard in this area as it is the core of our work. Please continue to beat into their heads that leadership is about being in control, about power and their ability to make quick decisions to protect the weak among them.

It almost seemed as if my student thought that he could work with his subject and allow him to bring about order without control. I am sure you would never have said this, but it is a reminder of the work you must do. This mentality has huge repercussions that we must be on guard against at all times.

Psychology 205: Distorting the subject's mind

I know our goal is to help our subjects see only single events or issues and polarize whenever possible, but my student actually had this problem. I cannot expect my student to train his subject if he is struggling with the same mentality. Let me repeat myself, it seems my student had the very problem I wanted to see in our subject. He was fixated on events and looking for a single cause that could explain it all. He could not see the deeper or longer-term pattern of events and seemed consumed with a short-term mentality. As an example, my student actually thought that one deliciously wrong choice by his subject was all that was needed to destroy his integrity.

As you will obviously understand, this mentality limited his ability to use our strongest and best weapon: a slow gradual process of decay that he doesn't notice is happening. I do realize our younger tempters are consumed with mass destruction and they do grow out of it, but please remind them that if there is an opportunity for mass destruction that Our Exalted Founder Below will take over immediately. This will sober them up quickly.

May I also ask you to remind your pupils that our subjects are easily capable of responding to a sudden crisis or changes that catch their attention and stir and challenge them. But they rarely have the tools to detect small changes over time.

One last thought in this area, please renew the research on the power of fragmentation and compartmentalization as a foundation for building single mindedness in our subjects.

Organizational Psychology 301:
Fundamentals of organizational death

I realize this course is built on Psychology 205, and both are linked together. I was disappointed with the limited knowledge of our historical attack on organizations that my trainee had. He acted as if it didn't matter. I know you would not promote this at all in your students. If this was the case I am sure you realize how short your time at the college would be.

I would strongly encourage you to give your students our latest manual of attack strategies. One of our core strategies is convincing the vermin to try and build 'learning' organizations, that the human scum don't have to learn but that the organization can. My student trainee had little awareness of how important organizational influence was and how much we could accomplish through it.

I think my student actually believed our lies to the vermin that organizations can learn. He knew little of how to create distance from the cause to the effect in an organization or even the basics of building a command and control hierarchy.

I am sure you were not aware of this lack of understanding in your students and that it will help you to continue your important work of developing future students who can destroy leaders and all those who follow them. May I recommend you retest your students to be certain they know our latest strategies?

Organizational Psychology 405:
The myth of unity

The students must be aware of the priority the enemy has on his subjects working together and how this is a condition upon his working through them. We must mislead with our tools

167

of conformity, externalization, belittling communication and pride.

Remind them not to let their subjects notice that those in the enemy's camp who are under persecution often operate in unity and don't even know it. Pound into them that success and greed are tools that distract those in the enemy's camp from this priority.

Graduate work: Ideas have consequences

This is an added note for those who want more graduate work in Deceiver's School. My trainee has forced me to rethink my own philosophy and the exalted wisdom of Our Founder Below, that ideas are the primary tools that we prepare the next generation of leaders to be bound by. I would be glad to come back and do some hands-on training with the other instructors there or pass on more extensive notes in this area.

I do believe that this will be a reminder of the work you are doing and need to do. I mean no disrespect for your work. I only send this as a reminder and in response to neglected areas I have seen in my work with my trainee.

Your ally in the war against our enemy,
Wyrmwud

The footnote from page 102.

[1] Barclay, W. (1960) *The Mind of Jesus*, London: SCM Press Ltd.

Interested in More?

AMuzement Publications

produces a series of books that captures the hearts of readers and provokes them to 'Muze' over who God is, who they are and the part they are to play in the world around them.

The Question
Is God good to all?
Who God is and how we view Him is The Question we are all confronted with at some point in our lives.

The Namer
God created us in His image. A primary part of that is our ability to give meaning to the world around us by naming it.

The Gate and other short stories
A collection of short stories that deal with: working together in unity called 'The Dance,' hardship called 'The Craftsman,' giving our gifts to God called 'The Song,' dealing with bitterness called 'Raising a Grudge,' and many, many more.

The Container
God made man complete in himself and yet incomplete alone. Why? He wants us to learn to build deep, lasting relationships that will provide a place for Him to dwell.

The Expression
Each person is made in the image of God and thus is a unique expression of God. What does it mean to have this expression within?

The Conversation
God created us to have an intimate relationship with Him. What are the ingredients in a good conversation with God? How can we learn to pray and touch His heart?

The View
"The View" explores different people's view of Jesus on the cross and how it affected them.

The Line
What part does the law play in our lives as Christians? In this story the law is described as a line that God has drawn for us not to cross. What happened when we did?

The Classroom
What if our world were a classroom and God was the master teacher?

The Choice
What part does our choice make in our Christian life and how is it an expression of humility?

These books will be available in the summer of 1999 and throughout the year 2000. Several other books on leadership and communication as well as short stories are in the works. They will be available at your local bookstores.

You may order the first three books and save a substantial amount. Check out ordering information on the next page for more details.

Contact us at:

info@amuzement.com

Our Web Site: **amuzement.com**
(You can order books directly from the web site.)

Address:
AMuzement Publications
7085 Battlecreek Rd. S.E.
Salem, Oregon 97301

AMuzement Publications
Order information

Our Price

The Question ($9.95 retail) $8.95

The Namer   ($10.95 retail) $9.95

Emails From Hell ($11.95 retail) $10.95

Shipping & handling
    Total for 1 - 2 books (U.S.A. Only) $3.00
    Each additional book (U.S.A. Only) $1.00
    Per Book   (International) $5.00

Special offer
Order all three books $26.95
(Includes shipping and handling - U.S.A. Only)

Make check payable to: AMuzement Publications
(You can order electronically at our website: amuzement.com)
Books can also be ordered through any bookstore.

Mail order and payment to:

AMuzement Publications
7085 Battlecreek Rd. S.E.
Salem, Oregon 97301

Please allow 2-3 weeks for delivery (International 4-6 weeks).
There is a volume discount of 25% on orders of 10 or more
books per title.

Printed in the United States
15690LVS00001B/106